Andhra Pradesh Priorities

Analysing costs and benefits

About Andhra Pradesh Priorities

The Andhra Pradesh Priorities project is part of the larger India Consensus – a partnership between Tata Trusts and the Copenhagen Consensus Center, which works to identify, analyse, rank and disseminate the best solutions for Indian states. The prioritization project unites the best academic research, employing cost-benefit analysis, with sector expert input, broad and inclusive stakeholder engagement, and extensive policy outreach, to evaluate and prioritise the smartest interventions.

For more information on the project, including the content of this book, please visit www.appriorities.com.

About Tata Trusts

Tata Trusts is amongst India's oldest, non-sectarian philanthropic organisations. The Trusts own two-third of the stock holding of Tata Sons, the apex company of the Tata group of companies. The wealth that accrues from this asset supports an assortment of causes, institutions and individuals in a wide variety of areas. In this manner, the profits that the Tata companies earn go back many times over to the communities they operate in. These funds have been deployed towards a whole range of community development programmes across the country, for over 100 years.

About Copenhagen Consensus Center

The Copenhagen Consensus Center is an award-winning think tank that researches the smartest solutions for the world's biggest problems and has helped policy-makers and philanthropists how to spend their money most effectively. Copenhagen Consensus has helped to focus billions of dollars of global aid and development spending on smarter priorities. The world's oldest academic publisher, Cambridge University Press, has published seven volumes of the Center's research.

ANDHRA PRADESH PRIORITIES

ANALYSING COSTS AND BENEFITS

BY

BJORN LOMBORG

SALEEMA RAZVI

BM NAIDU

ANDHRA PRADESH PRIORITIES

AN INDIA CONSENSUS PRIORITIZATION PROJECT

COPENHAGEN
CONSENSUS
CENTER

info@copenhagenconsensus.com
www.copenhagenconsensus.com

Cover design by: Rick Szuecs Design rickszuecs.com
Graphs and figures made with infogram.com, data source is the project research paper analyzing the respective interventions.

This work has been produced as a part of the Andhra Pradesh Priorities project under the larger, India Consensus project.

This project is undertaken in partnership with Tata Trusts.

TATA TRUSTS

Please cite the work as follows: Lomborg, Razvi and Naidu, Andhra Pradesh Priorities - analysing costs and benefits, Copenhagen Consensus Center and Tata Trusts 2019.

ISBN 978-1-940003-22-1

Contents

FOREWORD

BY RATAN N. TATA

For more than one hundred years, Tata Trusts have played a pioneering role in empowering, enabling, and transforming communities across India.

Through grant-making, direct implementation and co-partnership strategies, the Trusts support and drive innovation in areas as important as healthcare and nutrition; water and sanitation; energy; education; rural livelihoods; natural resource management; urban poverty alleviation; enhancing civil society and governance; media, arts, crafts and culture; and diversified employment.

Founder Jamsetji Tata's vision of proactive philanthropy is just as relevant today as it was a century ago, ensuring that the Trusts catalyse societal development with initiatives and interventions that have a contemporary relevance to the nation.

Today, spread over 17 states and 170 districts across the country, programmes supported by the Trusts reach out to millions of households through an efficient network of more than 450 partner organisations. Additionally, the Trusts' projects and initiatives, especially in the area of educational attainment, significantly contribute to capacity building across the country.

The Tata Trusts' collaboration with Copenhagen Consensus Center on the India Consensus project, which Andhra Pradesh Priorities is part of, is one of the ways that we are providing support for the development of innovation and intellectual capital, at the state level.

State governments are vital partners for Tata Trusts. Consolidated state government expenditure is now around 1.4 times the size of the Central government expenditure. With vision and judicious spending, states have the financial muscle to play a major role in the transformation of communities.

Given the breadth and diversity of India, every region has its own complexities, challenges, and opportunities, so solutions to challenges must be developed at a local level. But this does not mean that there is no role for world-class expertise or input.

The expectations placed upon state governments in this nation (and indeed on every state and national government in the world) are growing ever-greater. Quite rightly, citizens everywhere in the world demand better schooling and infrastructure, cleaner environment, and better-quality healthcare. Especially in the world's largest democracy, where free speech and free exchange are enshrined, these voices are powerful and important.

Indeed, for political decision-makers, one of the most important and weighty tasks is listening to the many different civic groups, looking closely at the challenges and opportunities ahead, and deciding carefully how and where to allocate limited resources.

No government or organisation on Earth is capable of meeting every last demand from citizens. The allocation of scarce resources can only be improved when decision-makers and the populace are provided with better information about spending choices.

This, indeed, is the starting point of the India Consensus project. This comprehensive undertaking provides a wealth of new economic findings, presented in this book, establishing what various interventions and initiatives can achieve in the state of Andhra Pradesh.

The benefits of the project are manifold, but the initiative particularly supports the Tata Trust's approach of fostering both innovation and intellectual capital.

The Trusts have long focused on innovative technologies and approaches to enhance the quality of life of communities. The focus has been on bringing in high-quality talent and technologies to speed and scale up interventions.

Tata Trusts have partnered with premier educational and technical institutions around the world, and like-minded multinationals, to design, develop and implement innovative programmes across different sectors such as education, digital literacy, health, livelihoods, and more.

The approach undertaken by Andhra Pradesh Priorities is entirely aligned with this approach: it is cutting edge analysis. It is particularly innovative to apply cost-benefit analysis across such a broad range of different spending options, at a state level. Very few governments or organisations undertake this important work, because it is so complvex.

Therefore, this approach itself breaks new ground, by standardising the academic approaches and ensuring that the costs and benefits of various policies can cohesively be understood together.

The contribution that Andhra Pradesh Priorities makes to boosting intellectual capacity is just as important to Tata Trusts. As Jamsetji Tata once said, "What advances a nation or a community is not so much to prop up its weakest and most helpless members, but to lift up the best and the most gifted, so as to make them of the greatest service to the country."

Some of the finest specialist economists from India have contributed academically to this project, giving their own service to the cause of identifying the social costs and benefits of various different approaches to challenges.

The findings of the Eminent Panel, published in this book, are a particularly important contribution because they highlight how thought leaders from India find that this research can be understood and interpreted, in ways that can lead to better decision-making. This contribution can only lead to a richer and more vibrant public discourse.

While the project has produced a wealth of innovative and informative findings, it is what happens next that is very important.

In that regard, this book is the opening of a conversation, rather than the end of one. The understandings between Andhra Pradesh Priorities and the state government has great potential to help translate this research and apply it in ways that will have a very important impact and will actually help to transform communities in effective ways. This would indeed be an enduring legacy of this project.

Mumbai, 23rd October, 2018

CONTRIBUTORS

Dr Bjorn Lomborg is president of the Copenhagen Consensus Center and visiting professor at Copenhagen Business School. The Copenhagen Consensus Center is a think-tank that researches the smartest ways to do good. For this work, Lomborg was named one of TIME magazine's 100 most influential people in the world. His numerous books include "The Skeptical Environmentalist", "Cool It", "How to Spend $75 Billion to Make the World a Better Place" and "The Nobel Laureates' Guide to the Smartest Targets for the World 2016-2030." In 2016, Prospect Magazine awarded Copenhagen Consensus Center, US International Affairs Think Tank of the Year.

Dr Saleema Razvi is the Senior Research Advisor for India Consensus and has anchored the Andhra Pradesh Priorities project in India. She has worked extensively on public health issues with the Population Foundation of India, Global Health Strategies, Digital Empowerment Foundation, National Council for Applied Economic Research, and Jawaharlal Nehru University. She has authored several research papers on the health sector in India and edited a book on the use of digital technology for healthcare.

Dr BM Naidu is Chief Consultant for the India Consensus project. He is a seasoned Monitoring and Evaluation Specialist with vast experience in health and social sector research. He served as a head of Monitoring and Evaluation divisions in several MNCs such as Cardno Emerging Markets USA Ltd., Futures Group International and Westat. He has published several research papers in scientific journals and prepared a number of project reports in health and social sectors.

Thank you to all economists and experts who contributed to the academ-ic research on costs and benefits under the leadership of **Dr Brad Wong** the Chief Economist of Copenhagen Consensus Center, and a specialist in social, economic and environmental benefit-cost analysis across development sectors.

The dedicated and enthusiastic India Consensus team consists of Dr. Manorama Bakshi, Amar Chancal, Dr. Paola Grenier, Steffi Itola, David Lessmann, Roland Mathiasson, Kuldeep Singh, Tejbir Singh and David Young with particular acknowledgement to the support provided by Pooja Parvati at Tata Trusts.

Panel of Eminent Economists

The Eminent Panel members met and put questions to the researchers at a three-day academic conference in Vijayawada in June 2018. The Eminent Panel comprises:

Professor Finn Kydland is a Norwegian economist known for his contributions to business cycle theory. He is the Henley Professor of Economics at the University of California, Santa Barbara. He also holds the Richard P. Simmons Distinguished Professorship at the Tepper School of Business of Carnegie Mellon University, where he earned his Ph.D., and a part-time position at the Norwegian School of Economics.

Professor Kydland was a co-recipient of the 2004 Nobel Memorial Prize in Economics, with Edward C. Prescott, "for their contributions to dynamic macroeconomics: the time consistency of economic policy and the driving forces behind business cycles".

Nisha Agrawal has worked on poverty, inequality and development issues for almost three decades. She was the Chief Executive Officer of Oxfam India, and worked with the World Bank on development issues for 18 years. Agrawal has experience working in countries in East Asia (Cambodia, Vietnam and Indonesia) and in East Africa (Tanzania, Kenya and Uganda). She has a Doctorate in Economics from the University of Virginia, USA. She has also worked as a Research Economist at the Impact Research Centre, University of Melbourne, Australia.

Vinita Bali is a global business leader with extensive experience in leading large Companies in India and overseas. She has worked with multinationals including The Coca-Cola Company and Cadbury Schweppes PLC, in addition to Britannia Industries Ltd., in India. She is a Non-Executive Director on the global boards of Smith & Nephew plc, and Bunge Limited; and Chairman of GAIN (Global Alliance for Improved Nutrition). She served on the Global Board of Syngenta International AG from April 2012 to June 2017. In India, Vinita serves as a Non-Executive Director on the Boards of CRISIL Ltd and Syngene International Limited; is a Member of the Board of Governors of Indian Institute of Management – Bangalore; and an Advisory Board Member of PwC.

Professor S. Mahendra Dev is Vice Chancellor of Indira Gandhi Institute for Development Research. He is Consultant and Adviser to many international organizations, including the United Development Programme, the World Bank, and the International Labor Organisation. Professor Dev was the Chairman of the Commission for Agricultural Costs and Prices, Ministry of Agriculture, in the rank of Secretary to Government of India from 2008 to 2010, and Acting Chairman of the National Statistical Commission of India in the rank of Minister of State. From 1999 to 2008, he was Director of the Centre for Economic and Social Studies in Hyderabad, India. He is President of the Indian Economic Association, Vice Chairman of Board of Trustees of IFPRI, and Chairman of the Committee on Terms of Trade on Agriculture constituted by the Indian Ministry of Agriculture.

ACADEMIC RESEARCHERS

Abhishek Kumar, CUG, Gandhinagar
Abusaleh Shariff, US-India Policy Inst.
Alex Golub, AU, Washington DC
Amitabh Kundu, RIS, New Delhi
Amitendu Palit, NU Singapore
Amit Sharma, The World Bank
Ankush Malhotra, UMTC
Anandajit Goswami, TERI
Arjun Kumar, IHD, New Delhi
Bjorn Larsen, Ind. Consultant
Bhawna Tyagi, IL&FS
D K Mangal, IIHMR, Jaipur
Dinesh Kumar, IRAP, Hyderabad
Eshita Mukherjee, DEF
Gaurav Bhatiani, IL&FS
Kaushik Bandyopadhyay, IIM, Lucknow
Kushal Sagar Prakash, Sunay Policy
Mansi Arora, Sunay Policy Advisory
Md Mahbub Hossain, IIHMR, Jaipur
Michael Murigi, Uni. of Sydney
Mrinal Chadha, NU Ireland
Munshi Sulaiman, Save the Children International
Nata Duvvury, NU Ireland
Neeraj Sharma, IIHMR, Jaipur
Nilanjan Banik, Bennett Uni., Delhi
Nim Pathy, Imperial College London
Nirupama Soundararajan, PIF
O Rajesh Babu, APUIAML
Parijat Dey, IL&FS
PR Sodani, IIHMR, Jaipur
Rajesh Chakrabarti, Sunay Policy Adv.
ReenaMithal, Sankhya Capital
Ritu Srivastava, DEF
S D Gupta, IIHMR, Jaipur
S V Subramanian, Harvard T.H. Chan School of Public Health
Shagun Khurana, Pahle India
Shreelata Rao Seshadri, Azim Premji University
Sonali Chowdhry, IL&FS y
SouvikBhattacharjya, TERI
Srinivas Raghavendra, NU Ireland
Surabhi Mittal, TARINA, TCI
Vijayalakshmi Hebbare, CGHR, Bangalore
William Joe, IEG, Delhi

ACADEMIC ADVISORY COMMITTEE

Dr Ashok Kumar Jain belongs to 1983 batch of Indian Forest Service, Telangana cadre. He is presently working as Adviser (Rural Development, Drinking Water & Sanitation, Housing, and Sustainable Development Goals) in NITI Aayog, Government of India. He did his M.Sc & M.Phil in Botany and Ph.D. in Development Studies. He has held several important assignments in Andhra Pradesh such as Divisional Forest Officer; Conservator of Forests; Project Director, Drought Prone Area Programme; Special Commissioner, DPAP & Wage Employment; Vice Chairman & Managing Director, Andhra Pradesh State Irrigation Development Corporation; Special Secretary, Irrigation & Command Area Development Department and Vice Chairman, Andhra Pradesh Housing Board & Commissioner, Housing. He is also a Member of several committees of Government of India.

Professor S. Galab is a Development Economist with a doctorate in Economics and Post Graduation in Economics and Statistics. Currently, he is Director of Centre for Economic and Social Studies (CESS), Hyderabad and leading the Young Lives, an International Longitudinal Project in Andhra Pradesh, on

Childhood Poverty. He has carried out research in fields of Rural Development and Agriculture on various aspects like Rehabilitation and Resettlement of Project Affected People, Natural Resource Management, Handloom and Power loom sector, Rural Indebtedness, Agrarian Distress and Farmers' Suicides, MGNREGS, and Dry Land Agriculture. He is a member of the Commission on "Inclusive and Sustainable Agricultural Development of Andhra Pradesh" constituted by Government of Andhra Pradesh.

Professor Faizan Mustafa is a senior law teacher and renowned jurist of constitutional law, who is presently working as the Vice- Chancellor of NALSAR University of Law, Hyderabad which is the country's leading National Law University and has emerged as the most sought-after destination of legal education in the entire South Asia. He has recently been unanimously elected as Vice President/ President-Elect of the prestigious Shastri Indo-Canadian Institute (SICI), which was incorporated in Canada in 1968 and is a bi-national organization of Canadian and Indian governments. Earlier, he was the Founder Vice-Chancellor of National Law University, Orissa.

Pavithra Kumar R heads the Tata Trusts operations in South India. He has been instrumental in putting together the team in AP and operationalizing the MoU signed with the State Government in 2015. He comes with 21 years of experience in the field of Finance and Social sector. Prior to joining the Tata Trusts, he was with Tata Communications Limited, Mumbai. He held positions in Corporate Finance, Strategy, Financial Planning & Analysis, etc. He was also part of the core team that involved in Global fundraising and Mergers and Acquisitions across the globe. He traveled widely across the world for delivering different assignments.

Professor Usha Vyasulu Reddy is currently Advisory Faculty at the Centre for IT and Public Policy, International Institute of Information Technology, Bangalore and has been a Visiting Professor at the S.N School of Communication, University of Hyderabad. She is a former Professor and Director, Centre for Human Development, Administrative Staff College of India, Hyderabad, and former Director, The Commonwealth Educational Media Centre for Asia, New Delhi. Earlier, she was Professor of Communication and Director, Audio Visual Research Centre, Osmania University.

Shri G. Sudhir, IAS (Retd) joined service in 1977 and served in the undivided state of Andhra Pradesh and held several important posts with distinction. He worked as Collector, Ranga Reddy and also Collector, Vizianagaram. From 1989 to 1994 he served in the Ministry of Human Resource Development and later Additional Development Commissioner, Handicrafts, Ministry of Textiles. After returning to the state in 1994 he served in Panchayat Raj & Rural Development Department, Higher Education Department, Cooperation and Agricultural Marketing Department, Tourism & Culture and also Finance Department. He retired as Spl. Chief Secretary Medical & Health Department in 2012. During his career, he had several important reforms in the respective sectors for the development of the state.

INTRODUCTION

BY BJORN LOMBORG AND SHIREEN VAKIL

Businesses, civil society and, indeed, every citizen has a stake in the important process of the Andhra Pradesh budget process, which sees roughly 1.57 lakh crore rupees allocated among important causes.

With some of the highest GDP growth rates of any Indian state, Andhra Pradesh is an important part of the nation's success story. But Andhra Pradesh, like every state and nation on Earth, does not have unlimited funds. It has to choose between many worthy opportunities to speed progress and respond to its remaining challenges.

What is the best way to continue developing while ensuring that everyone benefits, and gaps are closed? There are nearly as many different answers to that question as there are people living in the state.

For many, education is paramount – but does that mean first focusing on getting more people into tertiary education, or improving early childhood access, or on expanding skills training programs?

For others, the place to start is infrastructure. Some argue that health problems or social ills should be solved before tackling anything else. For yet others, the priority is strengthening institutions.

With finite resources, it is important for every decision-maker – not just in Andhra Pradesh but in every state and national government – to ask him or herself, how much will we achieve by spending that extra rupee on this policy or that? For example, what will we achieve by focusing on helping more people into higher education, and how much good will we achieve for Andhra Pradesh from spending the same amount on early childhood education? What social dividends will we reap from focusing on eliminating rural extreme poverty, and what will we achieve if we invest in expanding health packages?

Finding answers to these questions means creating knowledge and data that lifts the discourse and can lead to improved allocation of scarce resources.

Tata Trusts, one of the oldest non-sectarian philanthropic organisations, has been working with the think tank, the Copenhagen Consensus Center, to provide this very data. We have worked with many of Andhra Pradesh's top thinkers and influencers, including hundreds of sector experts, to find a wide range of views about the state's biggest challenges and most constructive responses.

Copenhagen Consensus has previously carried out research projects looking at global development priorities as well as national spending choices in Bangladesh and in Haiti. Our research– undertaken by some of the world's top economists, including Nobel laureates – has been used to inform the choices of UN agencies, philanthropic organisations, and governments.

The idea is to capture not only those that are 'hot' issues on the political agenda, but also to identify areas which might get less publicity – but where added focus could help to achieve a lot.

Encouragingly, there has been a lot of enthusiasm in Andhra Pradesh for the idea of cost-benefit analysis as a way to set priorities.

This project began with engagement across the state's vibrant policy, civil sector and academic circles. The project held 18 Sector Expert Consultations in Vijayawada, Guntur, Visakhapatnam & Hyderabad, where more than 600 policies and ideas that would improve Andhra Pradesh were discussed with over 220 experts.

This helped us focus on solutions to challenges which are important to the state and are worthwhile researching. This process identified dozens of solutions to study.

At a health sector expert roundtable meeting, for example, participants included representatives from Health & Family Welfare Department, Education Department, GoAP, UN agencies, private medical practitioners and health researchers from universities in India. This meeting alone identified 85 possibilities for further study.

Next, we asked an academic advisory committee, comprising Dr. Ashok Kumar Jain, Professor S. Galab, Professor Faizan Mustafa, Mr. Pavithra Kumar R, Professor Usha Vyasulu Reddy, and Shri G. Sudhir, IAS (Retd), to help to whittle this down to around 60 of the most promising ideas, and to sharpen the research focus.

We have then worked with some of the state's – and India's – top economists to analyze both the costs and the social benefits for each of these policies. In this booklet, much of their research is described.

Full copies of each of the research papers can be found and downloaded for free on the Andhra Pradesh Priorities website. In this book, each chapter tells its own story about opportunities to speed progress and continue to respond to challenges.

At the end of this book, are the findings of the Andhra Pradesh Priorities Eminent Panel. Nobel laureate in economics, Professor Finn Kydland is joined by leading economists Mahendra Dev, Vinita Bali, and Nisha Agrawal.

They gathered and interviewed all of the researchers and deliberated over the research, before agreeing on a list of the most effective investments. It is our hope that the research studies and eminent panel findings can provide inspiration for debate, and a valuable policy-making input.

None of this would have been possible without the hard work of the India Consensus team led by and Dr Paola Grenier, Pooja Parvati, and Dr Brad Wong in bringing this project to its logical conclusion. Dr Saleema Razvi along with the other team members Amar Chancal, Dr. Manorama Bakshi, Steffi Itola, David Lessmann, Roland Mathiasson, Dr. BM Naidu, Kuldeep Singh, Tejbir Singh and David Young did a phenomenal job in accomplishing results in a timely manner. A special note of gratitude to the state team of Tata Trusts in Andhra Pradesh led by Rajendra Babu who supported and facilitated the entire process.

In providing these findings in a book form, we hope that our conversation can broaden and help to ensure that thousands of crores of extra rupees of good can be created by virtue of sharpening the focus on the very best policies. This will ensure that more money and attention is devoted to the policies and interventions that will help Andhra Pradesh to write a bold new chapter in its admirable success story.

OVERVIEW OF THE SOCIAL, ECONOMIC AND ENVIRONMENTAL VALUE PER RUPEE SPENT

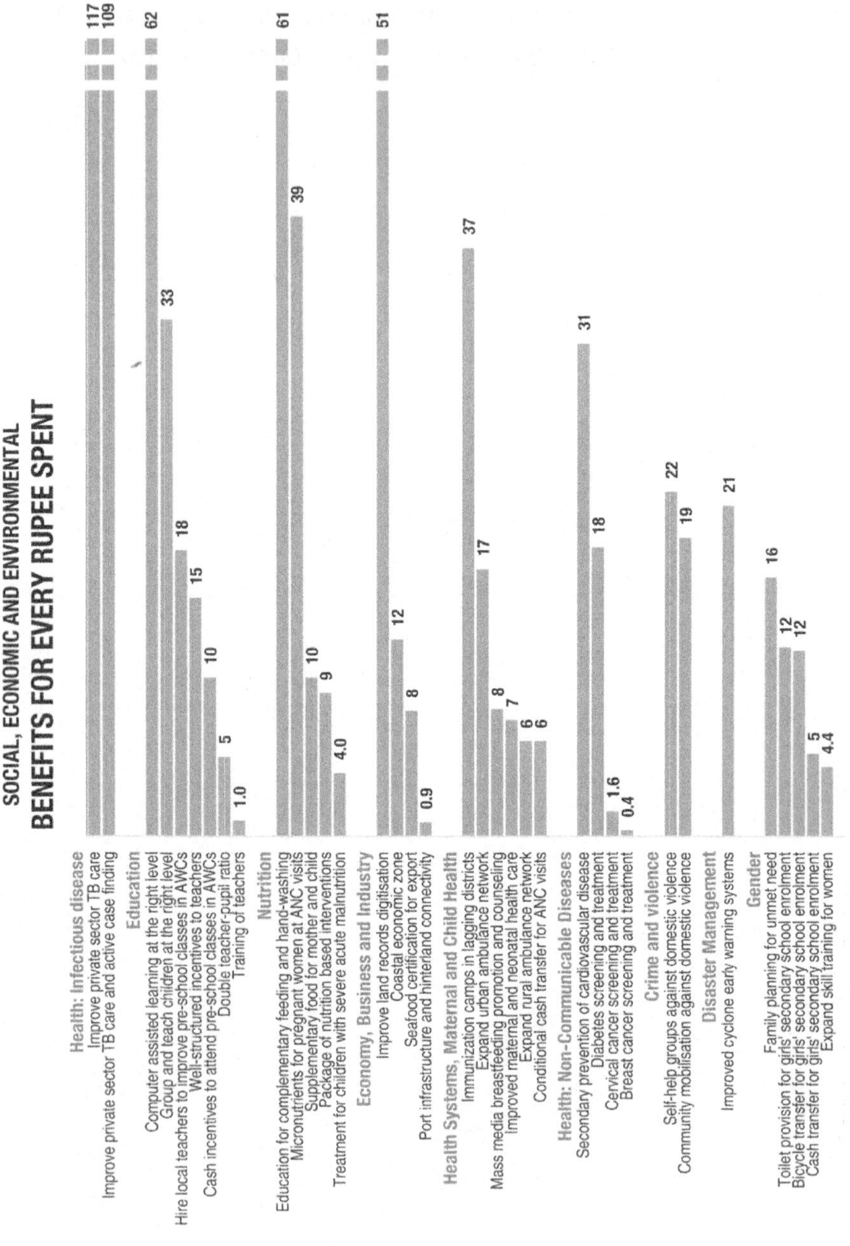
SOCIAL, ECONOMIC AND ENVIRONMENTAL
BENEFITS FOR EVERY RUPEE SPENT
Health: Infectious disease
Improve private sector TB care 117
Improve private sector TB care and active case finding 109
Education
Computer assisted learning at the right level 62
Group and teach children at the right level 33
Hire local teachers to improve pre-school classes in AWCs 18
Well-structured incentives to teachers 15
Cash incentives to attend pre-school classes in AWCs 10
Double teacher-pupil ratio 5
Training of teachers 1.0
Nutrition
Education for complementary feeding and hand-washing 61
Micronutrients for pregnant women at ANC visits 39
Supplementary food for mother and child 10
Package of nutrition based interventions 9
Treatment for children with severe acute malnutrition 4.0
Economy, Business and Industry
Improve land records digitisation 51
Coastal economic zone 12
Seafood certification for export 8
Port infrastructure and hinterland connectivity 0.9
Health Systems, Maternal and Child Health
Immunization camps in lagging districts 37
Expand urban ambulance network 17
Mass media breastfeeding promotion and counseling 8
Improved maternal and neonatal health care 7
Expand rural ambulance network 6
Conditional cash transfer for ANC visits 6
Health: Non-Communicable Diseases
Secondary prevention of cardiovascular disease 31
Diabetes screening and treatment 18
Cervical cancer screening and treatment 1.6
Breast cancer screening and treatment 0.4
Crime and violence
Self-help groups against domestic violence 22
Community mobilisation against domestic violence 19
Disaster Management
Improved cyclone early warning systems 21
Gender
Family planning for unmet need 16
Toilet provision for girls' secondary school enrolment 12
Bicycle transfer for girls' secondary school enrolment 12
Cash transfer for girls' secondary school enrolment 5
Expand skill training for women 4.4

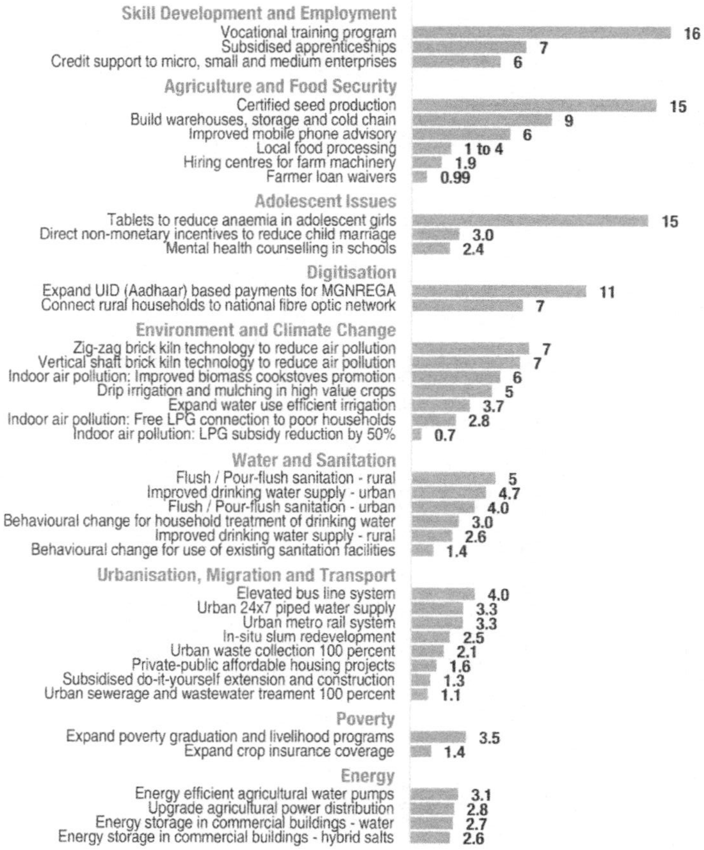

ANDHRA PRADESH PRIORITIES

AN INDIA CONSENSUS PRIORITIZATION PROJECT

All benefit-cost ratios are comparable. If you spend on promoting improved cookstoves, the social, economic and environmental benefits are 6 times the cost. Each rupee spent on expanded crop insurance will do 1.5 rupees of social and economic good.

In principle, all benefits are included. The benefits of providing family planning is not only avoided child and maternal deaths, but also increased growth from the demographic dividend.

Summaries and academic papers behind these numbers are available on www.appriorities.com

Adolescent Mental Health: An Underestimated Menace

Fifteen crore people in India are in need of mental health interventions and care, yet mental health is seldom part of the conversation on public priorities. Early intervention is particularly important: globally 10 to 20 percent of children and adolescents experience mental health disorders, and three-quarters of all mental illnesses emerge by the mid-20s.

Whilst the importance of physical health of adolescents, especially adolescent girls has been gaining ground in recent years, mental health remains a neglected and often taboo area.

Researchers SD Gupta, Md Mahbub Hossain, Neeraj Sharma, PR Sodani, and DK Mangal from IIHMR University, Jaipur, note that a lack of awareness about mental health often means that people do not access the services that they need, and only those patients with severe mental disorders are diagnosed and treated.

Untreated mental health conditions in adolescence can carry forward and worsen. It is extremely important to identify signs of trauma or disturbance and offer adequate counselling before these develop into a more serious condition requiring medication. Abuse and violence often cause trauma and mental health conditions, and evidence shows that domestic violence for instance is one of the strongest predictors of suicide amongst girls.

While there are gaps in the evidence on adolescent mental health, the 2016 National Mental Health Survey of India showed mental disorders among 7.3 percent of children aged 13-17, with prevalence in urban metros nearly double (13.5 percent) that of rural areas (6.9 percent). Major illnesses include depressive disorders (2.6 percent), disabilities affecting intellectual status (1.7 percent), agoraphobia (2.3 percent), autism (1.6 percent), psychotic disorders (1.3 percent) and phobic anxiety disorders (1.3 percent). Early recognition and intervention can improve outcomes.

Mental disorders in the age group 13-17

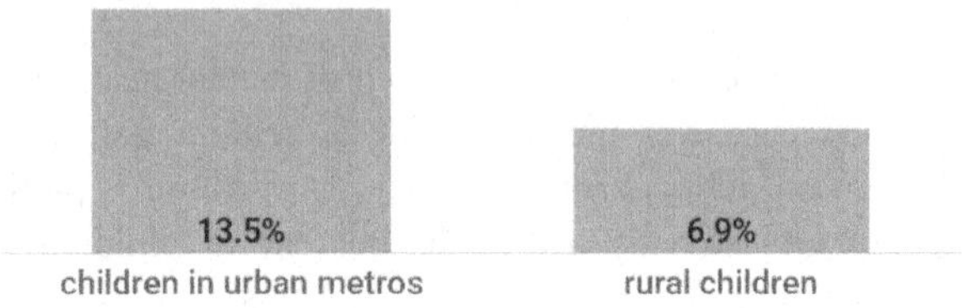

The researchers propose a screening, referral and treatment intervention for classes VI to XII at private and public schools, roughly covering children aged 11-17. Participation would be voluntary, requiring the consent of the adolescent and their parent or guardian.

Costs would include human resources for screening, material development and dissemination, along with clinical assessment, linkage to specialized care providers, and mental health services. In Andhra Pradesh, assuming that 80% of adolescents took part, enrolment and screening would reach 32.57 lakh young people, and about 5.86 lakh youths would be expected to require clinical evaluation. Including treatment for the roughly two lakh adolescents that would be anticipated to require it, the total annual cost of the intervention amounts to ₹122 crores.

In Andhra Pradesh, it is reasonably expected to stop about 164 young deaths from self-harm each year.

Mental Health also adversely affects the learning, education and social development of children. Interventions on this front would therefore also considerably reduce mental and physical disability, meaning that people can lead more fruitful, productive lives, and contribute more to society, including economically. The authors calculate that, put into monetary terms, all these benefits are worth ₹296 crores to the Andhra Pradesh economy.

Investment in adolescent mental health not only ‘breaks even’ but is a solid investment and generates returns to society worth more than two rupees for every rupee spent.

Adolescent physical health is also crucial, and the researchers highlight the benefits from focusing on anaemia, which affects many Indian girls.

Iron deficiency reduces physical fitness, which affects academic performance. In the long run, this affects maternal and child health and further increases the burden of disease.

A notable measure to address this challenge across India among 10 to 19-year-olds is the Weekly Iron and Folic Acid Supplementation which includes supervised consumption of iron and folic acid supplements with biannual deworming medications.

Anaemia cases averted due to the proposed intervention

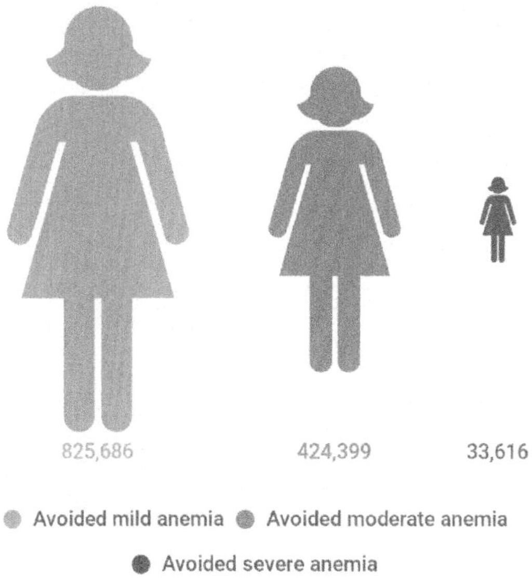

The researchers conduct a cost-benefit analysis for a program similar to this, but focused just on girls, for whom anaemia is a larger problem.

In Andhra Pradesh, more than 30 lakh adolescent girls suffer from anaemia, and 80 thousand from severe anaemia. The intervention is expected to reduce prevalence of all forms of anaemia from 69 percent to 40 percent, averting 13 lakh cases. With a total program cost of ₹44 crores each year, benefits would be worth nearly 15-times more.

This makes a strong case to take both adolescent physical and mental health seriously.

Interventions	BCR	Benefit	Cost
Preventing anemia among adolescent girls (annual cost)	15	₹655 crore	₹44 crore
Delaying child marriage via direct incentives (over 4 years)	3.0	₹4401 crore	₹1449 crore
School based behavioral screening and further mental health services for the adolescents (annual cost)	2.4	₹296 crore	₹122 crore

Total costs and benefits are discounted at 5%

Tackling Air Pollution by Cleaning Up Brick Manufacturing

With an average annual production of 200 billion bricks per annum, India is the second-largest producer of bricks in the world, after China. Over the last 40 years, brick production has increased more than 8 times, due to growing demand from the housing and infrastructure sectors.

Around 35 million tonnes of coal is consumed in the sector and is the third largest consumer of coal in the economy after thermal power, iron and steel. Brick is a major contributor to environmental pollution as it depends heavily on natural resources.

The predominant technology used for brick manufacturing in India is Fixed Chimney Bull's Trench Kiln (FBTK). This accounts for nearly 70 percent of the total brick produced in the country. However, other technologies that find application include Clamp Kilns, which produce bricks in batches where operation might be happening at relatively smaller scales, and are widely used in the peninsular region, contributing to about 25 percent of the total brick production.

The state of Andhra Pradesh is one of the key brick producing states in South India. The brick kilns in AP are located in six major districts which includes Krishna, Guntur, Vizianagaram, Srikakulam, Kurnool, and Ananthpur. Clamp kilns are the predominant technology for producing bricks in the state. The stacked raw bricks are irregularly fired with different fuels in between them. Since kilns are randomly designed, and are open, it leads to improper burning of the fuel as well as loss of heat thus making some bricks being over burnt and some unburnt leading to wastages.

Based on the estimates of the Global Burden of Disease methodology, Andhra Pradesh recorded more than 34,000 deaths due to exposure to PM 2.5. Further, an estimated 1,500 deaths have been attributed due to brick kilns in the state. There are variations in the average yearly concentration across six districts. For example, the highest average annual concentration has been observed in Krishna district, while the lowest average annual concentration has been observed in Vizianagram.

The economic and social benefit-cost assessment undertaken by economist Souvik Bhattacharjya, Fellow, Centre for Resource Efficiency and Governance, The Energy and Resources Institute (TERI), looks at two options for cleaner kiln technologies in the state of Andhra Pradesh. The two options involve improvement of existing Clamp Kilns and FCBTK to the Zig-Zag Kilns, and Vertical Shaft Brick Kilns (VSBK) technology.

Clamp kilns and/or Fixed Chimney Kilns can be converted to Improved Zig-Zag Kilns at low costs in the lowlands at the same site. This can be accomplished in less than half a year. The production capacity is the same or higher.

Benefits and costs of improved Zig-Zag Kiln technology

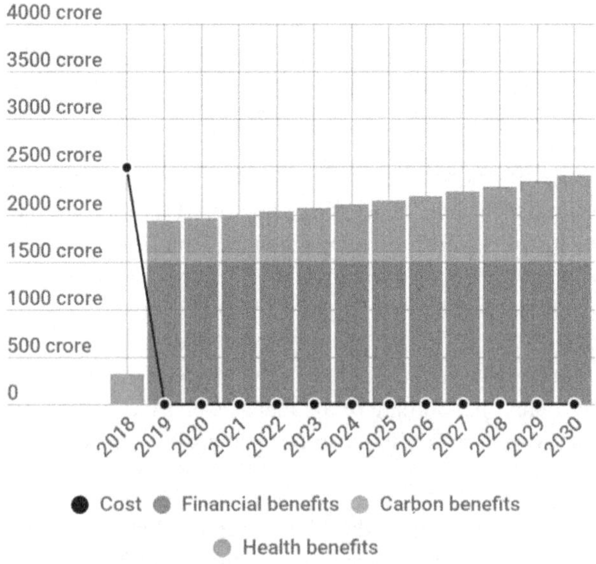

Zig-Zag brick manufacturing leads to 22 percent lower CO2 emission than Clamp kiln / Down draught kiln brick manufacturing process. It is estimated that the cost of the proposed intervention is approx. ₹2,496 crores.

The financial benefits have been estimated for a period of 12 years (till 2030). It has been found that the production of class 1 bricks can increase from 50 percent to 80 percent in case of Zig-Zag technologies.

The total incremental financial benefits are ₹12,673 crores till 2030. Further, with Zig-Zag technology, an estimated 7,552 deaths can be avoided (between 2019 and 2030), thereby improving quality of life.

This intervention would lead to total benefits worth ₹18,473 crores.

Vertical Shaft Brik Kiln benefits and costs over time

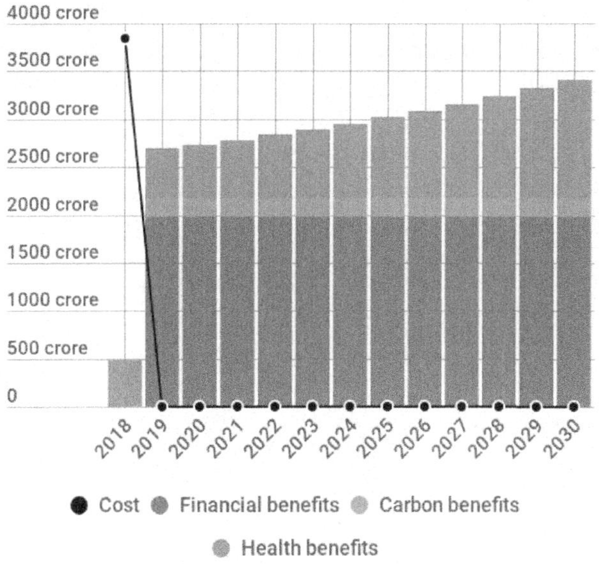

The VSBK technology uses hot exhaust gases for the gradual preheating of the unfired bricks in a continuous process, thus reducing energy consumption and CO_2 emissions compared to the more commonly used clamp kilns.

The total cost of this intervention is estimated to be approximately ₹3,840 crores.

Use of VSBK can lead to an incremental financial benefit of ₹16,725 crores. Retrofitting with VSBK technology is estimated to reduce CO_2 by 3.8 million tonnes.

The avoided CO_2 costs have been estimated to be ₹2,260 crores, and an estimated 11,528 deaths can be avoided, thereby improving quality of life between 2019 and 2030. The total benefits due to conversion to VSBK technology is ₹26,224 crores at 5% discount rates.

Interventions	BCR	Benefit	Cost
Improved Zig-Zag kiln	7	₹18,473 crore	₹2,496 crore
Vertical Shaft Brick Kiln technologies (VSBK)	7	₹26,224 crore	₹3,840 crore

Total costs and benefits are discounted at 5%

Agriculture and Water Resource Management: How to Boost Andhra Pradesh Farming

Two papers examine the best policies for Andhra Pradesh to pursue to reduce water scarcity and to improve agricultural performance.

One is by Dr Dinesh Kumar, Executive Director of the Institute for Resource Analysis and Policy (IRAP), Hyderabad, and examines policies to cut water scarcity in Andhra Pradesh.

In the Rayalaseema region, only about one-third of crops are irrigated, with the rest dependent on rain-fed cultivation, which is susceptible to the vagaries of the weather. Tanks are an important source of water for the rural economy, but – as in other areas – an explosion of well irrigation has reduced the surface runoff into these tanks. The biggest victims are poor, small, marginal farmers, who depend on tanks for providing supplementary irrigation for their kharif crop.

There are major water transfer projects being implemented. This approach – moving surplus water into the tanks, so that they are full – ensures farmers can continue crop production when the tanks do not receive inflows. According to one estimate, the additional storage space available during a drought year is about 1,700 million cubic metres.

The annualized cost of the infrastructure and drainage required to fill the tanks is estimated to be about ₹4,500 per ha, plus another ₹2,000 for annual operation and maintenance of the system. Assuming that the additional water will be used to irrigate around 65,000 hectares of under-paddy cultivated during winter, the overall annualized cost will be ₹43.2 crore.

Farmers will make more: the annual incremental net return is estimated to be about ₹9,000 per hectare. There would be further indirect benefits from energy savings because farmers wouldn't need to pump groundwater, and from the incremental return from the increase in the yield of wells and consequent expansion in the area served, and more intensive watering of irrigated crops. These benefits together add up to ₹15,000 per hectare per year, and the total annual benefits will be ₹159.2 crore.

This means that every rupee spent on the policy in Andhra Pradesh would generate benefits worth nearly four rupees.

Dr Kumar also examines investment in drip irrigation and mulching of high value crops, which would generate about five rupees.

Drip irrigation and mulch annual costs and benefits ₹/ha

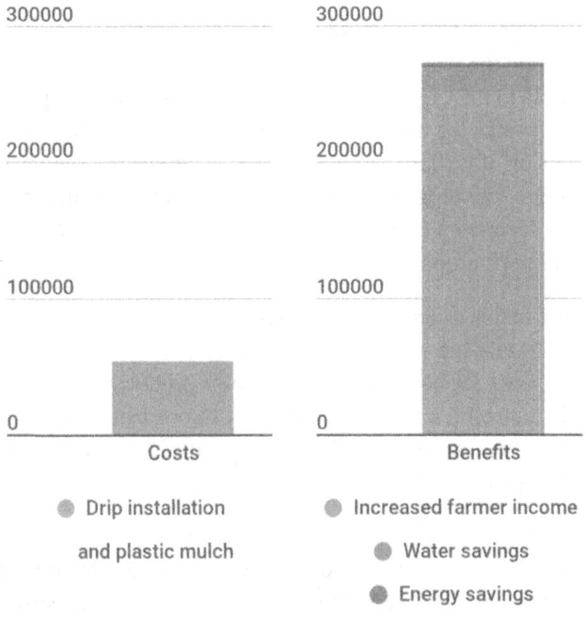

These are all respectable returns. But research by agricultural economist Dr Surabhi Mittal, Independent Consultant and Non-Resident Fellow, Tata-Cornell Institute for Agriculture & Nutrition (TCI), Technical Assistance and Research for India Nutrition & Agriculture (TARINA), suggests another approach may help farmers a lot more.

The researcher looks at various methods of improving farm productivity and farmer income, including improving farm mechanization through custom hiring services; improving extension services through the use of modern ICT tools; focusing on improving soil health; and improving the availability of certified seeds.

In India, farm-saved seed from previous crops remains the most prominent source of seed, year after year, accounting for nearly three-quarters of all seed usage. This means low crop productivity as optimal yield potential is a function of quality of seeds used.

Social and economic payback on agricultural interventions

Although a lot of improved varieties of seeds have been released for cultivation, their full impact has not been realized because of poor adoption rates and poor seed replacement rates.

The solution involves spending money on producing more quality seeds (for all the major crops in each state) and promoting this to farmers. The price-tag adds up to around ₹400 crores.

This will lead to better crop yields, increased production, and higher incomes. After reviewing the best evidence, the researcher suggests yield gains of ten percent can reasonably be expected with improved seed replacement rates. Even with this highly conservative assumption, the investment has huge payoffs: each rupee spent will have benefits to Andhra Pradesh worth around 15-times the costs.

These are phenomenal benefits and highlight the need to prioritize policies that will achieve the most for farmers.

Interventions	BCR	Benefit	Cost
Certified seed production and promotion	15	₹6,176 crore	₹401 crore
Improving/expanding extension services via mobile phones	6	₹6,250 crore	₹1,003 crore
Water saving through drip and mulching of 30,000 ha land	5	₹818.5 crore	₹161.3 crore
Irrigation expansion of 65,000 ha land through water transfer	3.7	₹159.2 crore	₹43.2 crore
Hiring centres for farm machinery	1.9	₹22,574 crore	₹11,892 crore

Total costs and benefits are discounted at 5%

Child Marriage: Tackling the Problem and Reducing the Insidious Impacts

While all agree that child marriage should be abolished, it continues, including in Andhra Pradesh, where the most recent National Family Health Survey (NFHS-4 2015/16) shows that 33% of women between the ages of 20-24 were married before age 18.

This has many insidious impacts. Girls that marry early typically stop going to school, meaning they receive less education, and are at a higher risk of domestic violence. In turn, their children receive less education. Child brides are much more likely to die in childbirth, and have worse health and nutrition, problems which are passed on to the next generation, who are more likely to be poor and unhealthy.

But how does Andhra Pradesh tackle child marriage? Clearly, outlawing the practice is not sufficient. We need to find targeted policies that will help a lot while remaining cost-effective. That is the goal of Reena V. Mithal, PhD, Managing Partner of Sankhya Capital.

Experience shows that the most effective policy interventions to reduce child marriage are based on the economic empowerment of girls through secondary education.

Dr Mithal examines four different policies that will reduce child marriage by boosting attendance at school for longer.

A typical barrier to girls' schooling is a lack of transport. Secondary school is often much further away than primary school. Without transport, more girls will stay at home, and will marry early.

Giving each girl starting in secondary school a bicycle may seem like an odd way to reduce child marriage, but it has been tested and found effective in Muralidharan and Prakash.

Over 4 years, the cost is 8488 rupees for each 14-year-old girl. About one-third of this is the cost of the bicycle, and the rest is basically the cost of the increased number of girls in school.

The policy will mean higher wages when girls graduate, because they will be better educated. Each year it will also mean 8,200 fewer girls child brides which has benefits for the girls, their children, and society. (The bicycle will even save transport costs, by itself almost worth the cost of the bicycle.)

Benefits of bicycle transfers to all eligible school girls age 14

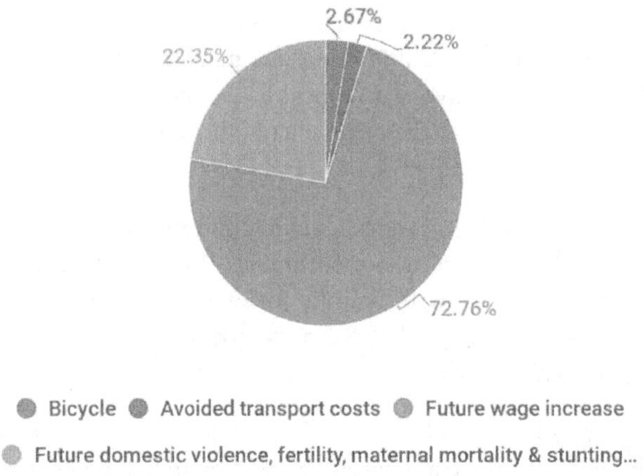

When all of these costs and benefits are compared, Dr Mithal finds that each rupee spent will generate ₹11.7 in benefits to society, with three-quarters of the benefits coming from the increase in girls' future wages

A lack of appropriate sanitation facilities also makes girls more likely to drop out. A recent survey in Andhra Pradesh found that 30% have a toilet problem: 4% have no toilets, 15% are not sex separated, and 11% are unusable.

Solving the problem means building around 580 new toilets, at a cost of 3.5 lakh Rupees each, spending 1.3 lakh rupees at each of about 2,000 schools to separate boy's and girl's toilets, and finally, spending 60,000 Rupees on repair at each of 1,500 schools.

Those costs plus maintenance add up to 82 crore in the first year, and 25 crore every year after that. Research shows the construction of a girls-only toilet increases upper primary school enrolment by 11%, increasing future wages, and reducing child marriage and all its attendant problems. In total, each rupee will generate 11.9 rupees of social good.

Dr Mithal also looks at the policy of using transfers to pay girls to attend school. This works well, but because it requires payments to everyone all the way through school, it is somewhat less effective, with a return to society of 5 rupees for every rupee spent.

This new economic data provides new inputs for decision-makers, by highlighting the returns that can come from investment in girls' empowerment.

Interventions	BCR	Benefit	Cost
Toilet provision for girls' secondary school enrolment (over 20 years)	12	₹19,294 crore	₹1,621 crore
Bicycle transfer for girls' secondary school enrolment (per cohort)	12	₹4,525 crore	₹387 crore
Cash transfer for girls' secondary school enrolment (per cohort)	5	₹5,714 crore	₹1,099 crore
Expand skill training for women (10 Lakhs young women)	4.4	₹2,272 crore	₹521 crore

Total costs and benefits are discounted at 5%

Digital Inclusion: Preparing for the Future

Digital inclusion has been the priority of the Government of India, with various efforts taken through the ambitious Digital India programme, including BharatNet Digi Locker, eSign Framework, National Scholarship Portal e-Hospital, and more.

The National Optical Fibre Network (NOFN) is an important component of Digital India. A fully operational NOFN has the potential of bringing significant changes to the lives of rural citizens.

National Optical Fibre Network (NOFN), an ambitious initiative to trigger broadband revolution in rural India, is creating a robust middle network infrastructure layer to connect gram panchayats of the country through broadband connectivity. NOFN has been planned with an investment of ₹21,000 crore to connect 2,50,000-gram panchayats with a speed of 100 Mbps. It was established to enable key services like e-governance, education, health, banking and agriculture in rural regions of the country.

There are several challenges in the deployment of NOFN, including a lack of accountability and delays in decision-making because of an emphasis on cost controls, resulting in poor implementation. There have been delays and increases in expenditure, unavailability of affordable devices, lack of available content, and limited affordability.

The progress in the NOFN has been slow in Andhra Pradesh connecting just 601 GPs out of 12918 GPs in the state.

Ritu Srivastava & Eshita Mukherjee of Digital Empowerment Foundation examine two options to build on India's digital inclusivity. The first of these is connecting the last sections of unconnected households via NOFN.

The cost is ₹10,179 crores, which includes: 1) cost of connecting the remaining GPs and ongoing maintenance; 2) cost to connect remaining households and ongoing maintenance; 3) upgrading the data centre cost to connect institutions (such as public health centre (PHC), schools, government agencies, etc) and 4) costs of accessing broadband services.

Cost over time to finalise the NOFN in crore rupees

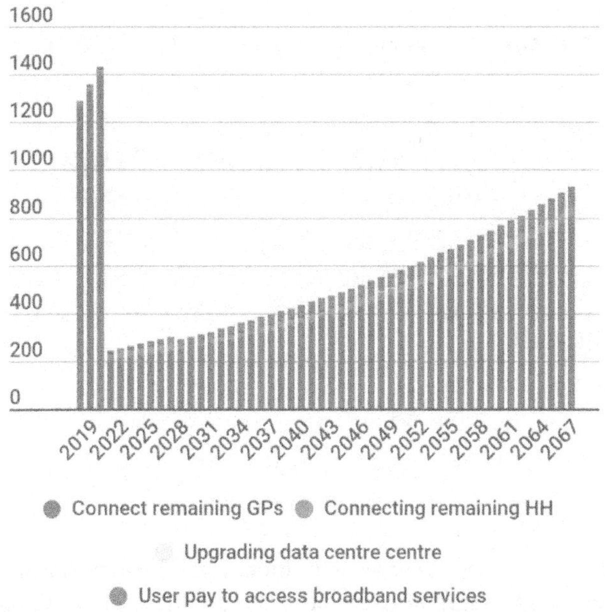

It is estimated that broadband penetration in rural Andhra Pradesh will increase to 38 per 100 rural households by 2067. Due to the falling share of rural population in the state, this will contribute to a statewide increase in penetration of 23 per 100 households.

The World Bank estimates that 10 percent increase in broadband penetration will lead to 1.38 percent increase in GDP growth on average for low/middle income countries. It is estimated that estimate there would be annual boosts to GSDP arising from the pathway of fixed broadband growth across the entire state attributable to the NOFN. After three years the boost to GSDP is 0.02%. By 2035 the boost is 0.1%, by 2050 the boost is 0.2%, and by 2067 it is 0.3%. Total benefits until 2067 equal 69,707 crores at a 5% discount rate.

The second option focuses on the Mahatma Gandhi National Rural Employment Guarantee Act (MGNREGA). MGNREGA promises to provide 100 days of wage employment to at least one member of the estimated 150 million rural households across India. However, there have been various implementation and service delivery issues since its inception.

MGNREGA workers and Aadhaar

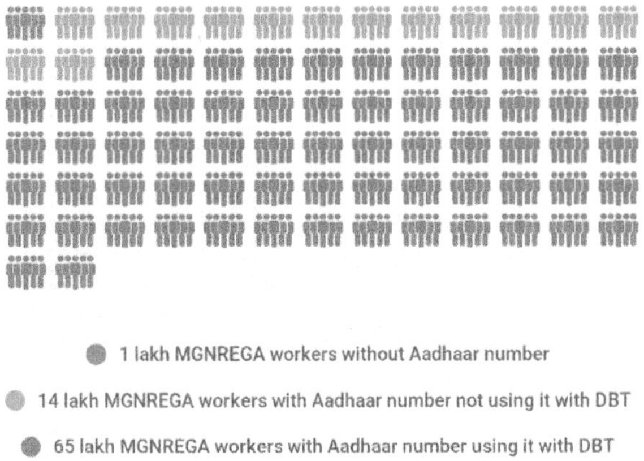

The intervention proposes transition from cash payment of MGNREGA wages to payment to the beneficiaries' bank/post office account linked to Aadhaar. Although 99 percent of the active MGNREGA beneficiaries have Aadhaar numbers only 82 percent receive their payments in their respective bank accounts. This intervention targets the last one percent of the population who are not linked to Aadhaar and those who are linked to Aadhaar but not linked to DBT.

The total cost of the intervention is ₹47 crores over a period of 15 years. Cutting down leakages is the key benefit of Aadhaar. The study estimates gain from reduction in two types of leakages a) leakages due to duplicity in the system b) leakages due to deception.

The gain from reduced leakages for total active MNREGS workers to be provided DBT (19%) is ₹57 crores.

Interventions	BCR	Benefit	Cost
Linking the last section of the un-connected MGNREGA population to Aadhaar	11	₹504 crore	₹47 crore
Providing the NOFN wired connectivity from gram panchayat (GP) to household (HH)	7	₹69,707 crore	₹10,179 crore

Total costs and benefits are discounted at 5%

Early Childhood: When Education Makes the Biggest Difference

Early childhood programs have long been shown to create improvements that last a lifetime. Whether by instilling good habits or by encouraging a passion for learning, early exposure to learning cuts drop-out rates in later schooling, and generates measurable improvements to the productivity and income of adults.

The Integrated Child Development Scheme, initiated in 1975 on a pilot basis, has now grown to include 1.3 million Anganwadi centres across the country – one of the largest initiatives of its kind in the world for children under the age of six.

But the big challenge for India is to expand pre-school education access to even more children, and – crucially – to lift the quality of education offered.

Most Anganwadis operate primarily as nutrition or day-care centres with no staff formally trained in child development. Only half have basic tools for learning, like appropriate books, drawing materials, and puzzles, the government found in 2011. More than three-fifths of staff receive no help from supervisors to plan or execute educational activities, according to one recent study.

Abusaleh Shariff, Chief Scholar of the US India Policy Institute and Amit Sharma, Consultant with the World Bank in New Delhi and People Research on India's Consumer Economy, conclude that there would be significant benefits from focused investment in early childhood education.

First, they analyse the effectiveness of cash incentives to expand access further. Cash vouchers have lifted pre-school attendance in rural China. Using a similar incentive structure in Andhra Pradesh, they find this would be equivalent to offering about ₹6,000 to the family of a four-year-old to attend pre-school education programs at Anganwadis in the state, regardless of the parents' income. The total cost for Andhra Pradesh would run to about ₹333 crore per year.

Such an incentive will likely result in a 35% increase in preschool enrolment, taking enrolment to 66%. This will lead to an addition of 1.4 lakh new 4-year-olds to the state's Anganwadi preschool education program.

Cash incentive vs. lifetime wage benefit from pre-school

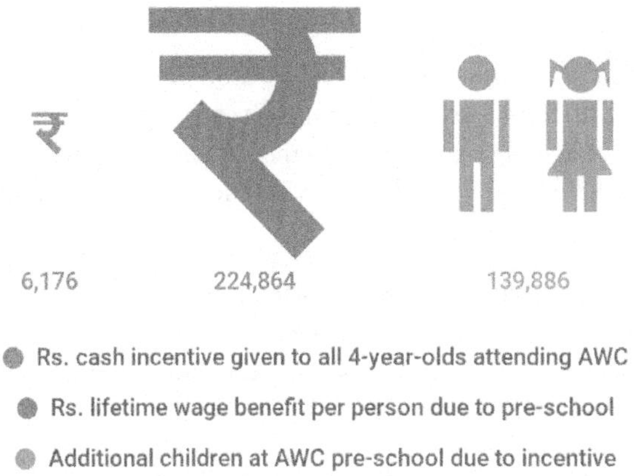

Early learning can help increase later academic achievement, build a desire to learn and aid better social and emotional development. Perhaps the most well-established result is that access to preschool education translates into an increase in future wages. Even using a conservative approach of only identifying how much more children will earn given a year of pre-school education than those who remain illiterate means an average wage increase of 23% when children grow up. For each child helped, that means more than two lakh rupees over a lifetime, or ₹3,146 crore for all of Andhra Pradesh. In all, every rupee spent would generate benefits worth 10 rupees to society.

This approach would expand access. But how can India lift the quality of preschool education in Anganwadis? The authors look at a model already being used successfully in Karnataka. This would see spending of about ₹7,000 per year on each child aged 3-6 years enrolled in Anganwadis, on improving the quality of preschool education.

They suggest partnering with accredited localized organizations that focus on early childhood education and development, such as the Hippocampus Learning Centers in Karnataka.

This would be enough to hire one teacher per centre, improve the curriculum, train existing Anganwadi staff, and provide uniforms and books for students. One teacher would come to the centre every day for one year.

The effect of this intervention is based on the demonstrated effectiveness from private school preschool programs. While private preschools are not perfect, they are generally regarded as providing a more appropriate environment and curriculum for children than Anganwadis.

Bringing the quality of preschool education provided through Anganwadis to a level with private preschools would cost about ₹1,183 crore per year for all the 3-6 year-olds currently enrolled at Anganwadis in Andhra Pradesh.

The researchers' analysis concludes that this would lead to a 13% increase in average wages for the children when they grow up, a present value of ₹1.3 lakh per child. With a cost of ₹7,000, that means each rupee spent on higher quality education generates a very generous return of ₹18.

Investment in expanding early childhood education access and improving quality would transform lives for many years to come.

Interventions	BCR	Benefit	Cost
Improving quality of PSE by partnering with localized organizations	18	₹21,815 crore	₹1,183 crore
Conditional payments for 4- year-olds to attend PSE classes at AWCs	10	₹3,479 crore	₹333 crore

Total costs and benefits are discounted at 5%

Education Policies to Help Andhra Pradesh Achieve its Full Potential

To achieve its full potential, it is crucial that India enacts education reforms to enhance human capital. Government policies have so far lifted school enrolment and retention rates.

While more children are staying in school for longer, Pratham reports show challenges with learning outcomes: in 2005, 49 percent of Grade 5 students could do division; by 2016, it was 26 percent. Only half of children in Grade 5 can read a Grade 2 textbook.

Dr Rajesh Chakrabarti and Kushal Sagar Prakash of Sunay Policy Advisory have examined the efficiency of various education policies.

First, they look at two interventions consistent with the Right to Education Act: in-service teacher training, and reducing pupil-teacher ratios.

The authors find that even lengthy, in-depth tertiary courses and pre-service training of teachers have been found to have zero to modest effects on student learning outcomes, so it seems very unlikely that in-service training, which only occurs for a few days each year, would achieve any more.

Training costs just ₹372 per student annually – but the researchers conclude the policy is unlikely to generate benefits in student outcomes that are worth more to society than the cost.

Likewise, a simple analysis finds that halving the pupil-teacher ratio in Andhra Pradesh is expensive compared to other approaches, costing ₹13,455 per student, generating benefits to learning outcomes that, in an optimistic scenario, are worth five-times the costs.

The researchers also examine ideas that are not yet official government policy but have been tested across India, including in Andhra Pradesh.

The first of these is providing performance-based incentives to teachers: effectively, paying teachers more when learning outcomes improve the most. A trial in Andhra Pradesh cost ₹552 per student per year, and resulted in better student test scores, with no evidence of any adverse consequences.

Test-score gains are linked to higher productivity in adulthood, and the researchers calculate the net effect as a 7.3 percent boost to students' wages. These concrete benefits to society are worth 15-times more than the costs of the intervention.

Next, the study examines 'teaching at the right level', which does away with grade-level curriculum and involves organising children into groups based on their current learning levels.

Lifetime values of teaching at the right level

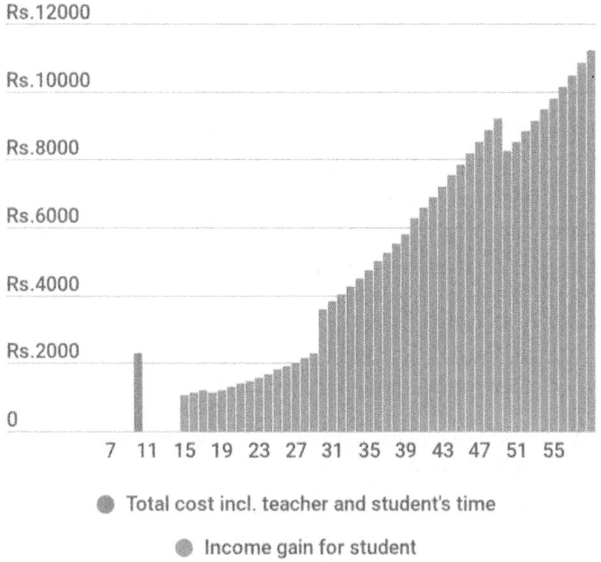

Pioneered by Pratham in India, it is deployed in two ways. The first approach involves running intensive camps, usually 80-100 hours long, with trained Pratham staff and community volunteers. The second approach involves partnership with government to embed the intervention at scale across one or more districts. Teaching at the right level can be done either outside or within existing school time.

Depending on which approach is used, the intervention generates lifelong benefits to students' incomes worth at least 21-times the costs, and up to 44-times the costs in the right conditions.

Value of future wage increase vs. cost per student in ₹

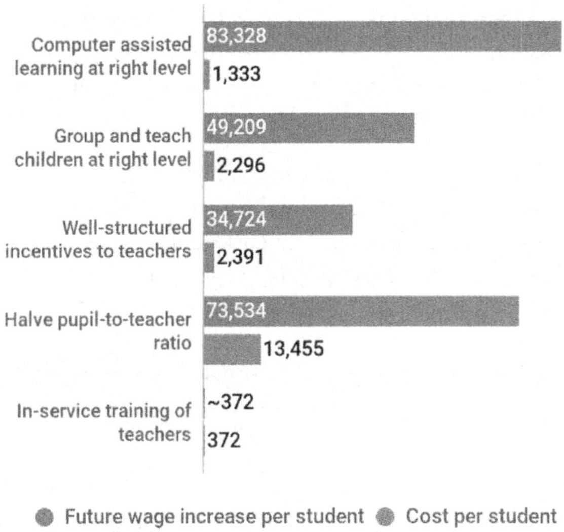

Finally, the authors examine computer-assisted learning, which uses technology to help students learn at their own level. Mindspark is one such personalised technology intervention, implemented in a rigorously measured program over five months in three low-income schools in Delhi.

Adapting this program for fifty schools, and including infrastructure, hardware, staffing and software development, would cost about ₹1333 per student over five months.

Several studies into Mindspark have shown improvements in student test-scores, and have revealed that there may be large returns to further innovation and research on effective ways of integrating technology-aided instruction into classrooms

After five months of access to the program, one robust study showed students scoring 14% higher in mathematics and 9% higher in Hindi relative to the students who didn't have access to Mindspark.

Plenty of research shows how much future wages are influenced by higher test scores. With these results, the researchers find that on average each student will make ₹83,328 more over their lifetime. Spending just ₹1,333 per student to achieve such an impressive result means every rupee spent would generate benefits to society worth ₹62.

It is policies like these that India must embrace, to fully reap its demographic dividend. Getting children into classrooms is no longer enough. Investment in low-cost, high-impact education that will make students more productive is vital.

Interventions	BCR	Benefit	Cost
Computer assisted learning	62	₹83,328 /student	₹1,333 /student
Teaching at the right level without an extra hour	44	₹49,209 /student	₹1,108 /student
Teaching at the right level with an extra hour	21	₹49,209 /student	₹2,296 /student
Performance based incentives to teachers	15	₹34,724 /student	₹2,391 /student
50 percent reduction of pupil teacher ratio	5	₹73,534 /student	₹13,455 /student
In-service training of teachers	~1	~ ₹372 /student	₹372 /student

Total costs and benefits are discounted at 5%

Reducing Electricity Sector Losses to Power India's Future

Inadequate and poor quality power supply means frequent interruptions, poor voltage levels, and dissatisfied consumers across much of the country.

Adding up all the losses in the system – including the losses due to energy dissipated in conductors, transformers and other equipment, along with pilferage by those who bypass meters, and losses from failure to recover the amount billed to consumers – India's total energy losses came to 24 percent in 2015-16, significantly more than international norms.

This, however, is an improvement on 2003-04 when the same losses were 38 percent. Progress was made because of national and state level reforms.

Dr Gaurav Bhatiani, Chief Operating Officer, IL&FS and his colleagues Bhawna Tyagi, and Sonali Chowdhry look at state-level solutions.

They zeroed in on the agriculture sector, one of the most inefficient electricity users. In the 1960s, the rural electrification programme was introduced to enhance agricultural output using groundwater for irrigation.

Due to un-metered supply and the flat rate electricity tariff provided for irrigation, the number of pumpsets increased substantially – and unregulated and free water has contributed to over-exploitation of groundwater resources. Subsidised power intended to benefit farmers allowed problems such as pilferage and theft, and disguised losses from the utilities, which degraded their finances.

The ultimate burden of losses is on the State Governments which collectively spent ₹36,758 crore in FY 14, ₹45,584 crore in FY15 and ₹55,283 in FY 16 (annual growth of 23%) on subsidising utilities for supplying low cost electricity for irrigation.

One of the major reasons for the high losses was the adoption of a low-tension distribution network spread over long distances to serve dispersed, small, individual agriculture connections. This resulted not only in high technical losses, but also in theft facilitated by unmetered supply and the flat tariff.

The degradation of the utilities' finances has adversely affected farmers by making the supply and quality of power unpredictable and by providing it mainly during the night hours. This resulted in frequent failure of pumpsets, forcing farmers to use inefficient motors, and keep the pumpsets constantly on, wasting energy and overexploitation of groundwater.

All in all, this is a vicious cycle in which farmers, distribution companies, and State Governments alike all face ever-increasing losses.

The researchers propose two solutions. The first is to introduce a high-voltage distribution system (HVDS), by upgrading the network and replacing transformers.

Andhra Pradesh has already made a strong start on conversion of LT network to HVDS and managed to reduce losses to 12 percent, demonstrating that this approach works. Completing the upgrade would cost ₹7,147 crore. The biggest saving would come from the fact that pumpsets wouldn't fail so often. That alone would be worth ₹18,944 crore.

Factoring in carbon savings, energy savings, and the reduction in transformer failure, the total benefits would come to ₹20,028.

In short, each rupee invested would generate a return worth more than two rupees.

The second solution proposed by the researchers i.e. replacing inefficient pumpsets with energy efficient ones further enhances the return on investment.

The total costs would be almost twice as large, because we would need not only the high-voltage distribution system to be set up, but also replace all existing pumps. Yet, the total benefits would grow even more, allowing each rupee to generate three rupees of social benefits, both through lower pump breakage, along with energy savings and carbon savings. Both these interventions will also result in a significant indirect benefit by enabling reduction in the subsidy by Governments for irrigation amounting to at-least ₹3,000 crore, which can be redirected to other areas.

Crore ₹ costs and benefits of agricultural power upgrade to high-voltage and installing energy efficient water pumps

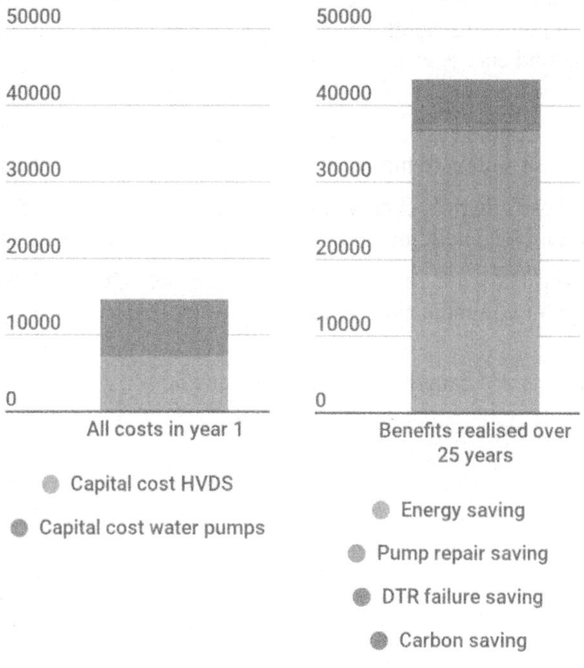

Anandajit Goswami of the TERI School of Advanced Studies, and Kaushik Ranjan Bandyopadhyay of the Indian Institute of Management examine rising energy demand in buildings, which is accompanied by a rise in electricity use leading to a rapid increase in carbon emissions and aggravating power shortages. They show the benefits of using water- or salt-based thermal energy storage in buildings, and find the investment would have a return worth more than two rupees for every rupee spent.

This highlights both the lasting challenges that can be caused by well-meaning policy decisions such as the low-tension distribution network and introducing energy efficient pumpsets but also the opportunities that exist to reduce losses in the power sector. This would be a win-win for everyone.

Interventions	BCR	Benefit	Cost
HVDS and EEPS - Upgrade agricultural power distribution to high voltage and energy efficient agricultural water pumps	3.1	₹43,294 crore	₹14,164 crore
HVDS - Upgrade agricultural power distribution to high voltage	2.8	₹20,028 crore	₹7,147 crore
Water based thermal energy storage for commercial buildings	2.7	₹1,448 /sq. ft.	₹531 /sq. ft.
Salt hybrid based thermal energy storage for commercial buildings	2.6	₹1,448 /sq. ft.	₹566 /sq. ft.

Total costs and benefits are discounted at 5%

EXTREME WEATHER: SAVING MORE LIVES IN CRISES

When extreme weather strikes, even relatively small productivity shocks can cost societies dearly. Yet there is considerable diversity across India in terms of preparedness for natural disasters: In coastal Odisha, 99% of the population is aware of the comprehensive early-warning system. Yet in Andhra Pradesh, which is very vulnerable to tropical cyclones, about 30 percent of the exposed population is not aware of the early-warning system.

Proportion not responding to early cyclone warnings

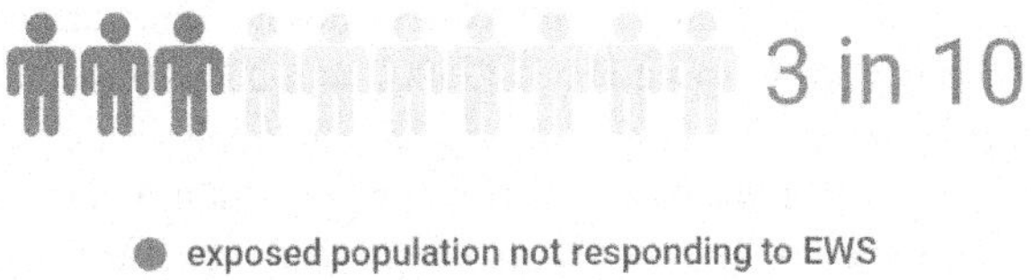

Alex Golub from American University and Elena Golub highlight the advantages to be gained by ensuring that inhabitants of Andhra Pradesh are just as prepared for natural disasters as those of Odisha.

Since the Diviseema cyclone of 1975, Andhra Pradesh has weathered more than 60 cyclones, some of them moderate and some ferocious. These include the May 1990 severe cyclonic storm with a core of hurricane winds that claimed 817 lives, damaged 1.4 million houses and ruined more than 500,000 hectares of crops, with total damage amounting to ₹2,137 crore. And the November 1996 severe cyclonic storm that hit four districts, claiming 1,077 lives, damaging 600,000 houses and wiping out 500,000 hectares of crop, with a total price-tag of ₹6,129 crore. And Cyclone Laila in May 2010 only killed 22 people but damaged 14,298 houses, wiped out 260,000 hectares of crops, and led to total losses worth ₹1,603 crore.

A lack of preparedness matters. According to research, a vast number of deaths and a large percentage of material damage could be avoided if proper actions are taken in a timely manner.

With 12 hours lead time, almost all natural disaster-caused fatalities in Andhra Pradesh could be avoided if the early warning system preparedness was at the same level as Odisha, along with about 40 percent of material losses. This includes livestock which can be moved, but excludes crops, because an early warning system is unlikely to be able to prevent those from being damaged.

The Golubs look into the cost of strengthening village implementation of the states' early warning system, by building awareness among communities to act upon the warnings to mitigate the losses.

The authors assume that every four years, each household receives an emergency kit (costing about ₹2500), and one representative from each household should participate in training (which costs them a day's income). Also, for every 100 community members, two leaders should undertake more intensive training on a regular basis for so as to build awareness about any changes in the system over time (costing around ₹38,500 for every 1,000 people in the population). Finally, a community communication (warning system) should be maintained and upgraded (at an estimated cost of around ₹83,000 per 1,000 residents).

Of course, the system won't work all the time – indeed the authors estimate that 30% of damages will still be lost. Moreover, there will be false alarms, which each cost a day's work, but will save nothing at all. Yet, when the early warning systems work, they will prevent almost all fatalities, most livestock loss, and some damage to houses.

Adding all of these benefits together, the incremental benefit from getting Andhra Pradesh's preparedness to the same level as Odisha means avoiding losses to society worth in the region of ₹1.2 lakh crores over the next 35 years. This means that every rupee spent on the intervention would generate benefits to Andhra Pradesh that are worth 20 rupees.

Simulated preventable damage from a tropical cyclone in Andhra Pradesh and probability of event occurring

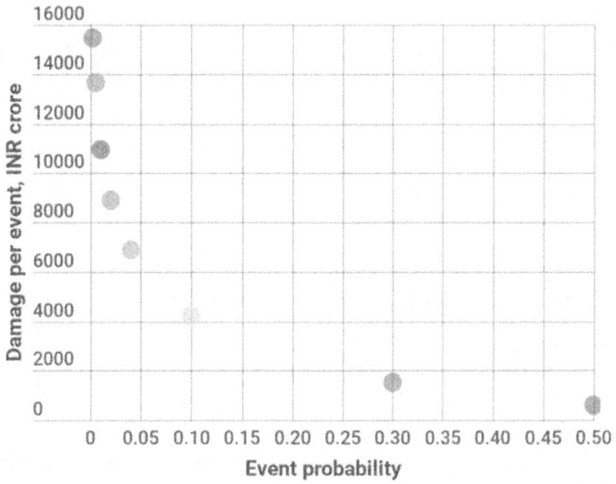

Improving disaster preparedness very importantly saves lives, but it also helps save livelihoods, making sure that entire communities are not financially wasted by the vagaries of nature. While any early warning system is no substitute for far-reaching adaptive measures to try to reduce the harm done by nature, making sure that inhabitants are prepared for the worst is simple common sense.

Interventions	BCR	Benefit	Cost
Community level improvement in cyclone early warning system (total costs over 35 years)	20.8	₹119,724 crore	₹5,747 crore

Total costs and benefits are discounted at 5%

The Real Strategies to Reduce Farmer Distress

In Andhra Pradesh, promising policies could help to reduce farmer distress.

About three-quarters of land holdings are less than two-hectares, meaning farmers cannot reap economies of scale. This exposes farmers to natural disasters, droughts, and price fluctuations.

Professor Nilanjan Banik from Bennett University, Greater Noida studied responses to farmer distress. Andhra Pradesh has one of the highest national rates of farmer suicides, with 47 self-inflicted deaths per 1000 population between 2010 and 2012.

Last year, Uttar Pradesh, Maharashtra and Punjab undertook large-scale farm debt waivers, costing half a percent of the entire GDP of India, and Andhra Pradesh itself has recently announced a loan waiver costing ₹24,000 crore.

However, the research by Professor Banik, supported by other economic studies, finds that a loan waiver scheme costs about as much as it achieves. Moreover, it mostly helps richer and bigger farmers, leaving smaller farmers worse off in the future.

Only 15% of the marginal farmers (with less than 1 hectare of landholding) have access to formal credit, so a loan waiver helps them little, and previous waivers have led to banks reducing credit for small farmers.

Professor Banik's analysis for Andhra Pradesh shows that waiving formal loans for land holders with less than two hectares would cost ₹24,860 crores. The benefits will be slightly lower at ₹24,629 crores. Giving out a rupee to achieve just 99 paise of benefit is a poor deal. It also means a 15% reduction in smallholder credit over the following years, cutting revenue for the most vulnerable farmers by 13.5%. And spending thousands of crores on less effective policy leaves less for much more effective ones.

Total formal credit held by farmers

But other interventions could be much more helpful. For Andhra Pradesh, the research suggests that one answer is reducing waste of perishable fruits, vegetables and milk that command a higher market price than staple crops. Most small farmers do not risk growing perishable crops. Nearly 20% of India's fresh produce is wasted because of storage problems.

The National Centre for Cold Chain Development (NCCD) estimated AP's total requirement for storing milk, fruits and vegetables at 744,650 metric tonnes last year. Meeting this need would help farmers shift to high-return crops, which lowers their likelihood of poverty by 3-7%. Costs, including employees, storage, packhouses, and trucks, come to about ₹11,482 crores annually. The benefits in terms of the reduced wastage in milk, fruits and vegetables, are worth nearly nine-times that figure.

Farmer distress requires a serious response – but as in everything, there are choices. Economic analysis clearly shows that each rupee could achieve stronger benefits by focusing on solutions such as improving cold storage.

Interventions	BCR	Benefit	Cost
Farm loan waiver (Time horizon 5 years)	0.99	₹24,629 crore	₹24,860 crore
Cold chain infrastructure (Time horizon 10 years)	9	₹101,451 crore	₹11,482 crore
Local food processing (Time horizon 1-3 years)	Approx. range 1-4	Depends on local conditions & type of processing	Depends on local conditions & type of processing

Total costs and benefits are discounted at 5%

Reducing Domestic Violence Would Have Vast Economic Benefits

Andhra Pradesh would enjoy an economic boon worth thousands of crores of rupees if it steps up efforts to reduce domestic violence.

Globally, violence between intimate partners is huge: it costs the world 25-times more than all wars and terrorism. In India, the latest National Family Health Survey shows that 22 percent of married women aged 15-49 experienced spousal physical or sexual violence in the past 12 months. That suggests that in India, at least five crore women were assaulted last year.

Violence against women the past year

Yet, there has been relatively little research into reducing this devastating impact. Despite nearly a decade of implementation, evidence of the effectiveness of the 2005 Domestic Violence Act is fragmentary at best. The few available assessments suggest there is a lack of clarity within the judiciary about interpretation, inadequate money is allocated to establish required infrastructure, and there is too little awareness about the law among judges, protection officers and civil society, as well as among women.

It is clear that legislation alone is not enough to change outdated norms that underpin violence.

Research from Srinivas Raghavendra, Mrinal Chadha, and Nata Duvvury of the University of Ireland Galway helps close gaps in the evidence – and points to sizable economic benefits from reducing domestic violence.

The researchers study two of the very few approaches that there is empirical evidence of effectiveness.

The first is based on the *SASA!* project, which is a community mobilisation intervention seeking to change the norms and behaviours that result in gender inequality, violence and increased HIV vulnerability for women, pioneered in Uganda and used in more than 20 countries.

The approach, costing ₹980 per person, guides communities through a process in which people are repeatedly exposed to the programme. New attitudes and norms that promote more equitable relationships diffuse throughout the community.

The researchers suggest that this community mobilisation intervention could target women aged 15-59 years below the poverty line who have been in a partnership in the past year. In Andhra Pradesh this would mean reaching 17 lakh women for a price-tag of ₹164 crore.

Of these 17 lakh women, more than 5 lakh would be assaulted by a spouse annually. Based on studies in India and abroad, it is likely each of these women will on average experience abuse 8-times a year.

The second intervention, used in South Africa, combines microfinance with training about domestic violence, gender norms and sexuality, thus providing women with the means and knowledge to improve their well-being.

The study explores the effects of using the intervention to target the same women over a two-year trial, followed by a two-year scale-up. It would cost about ₹850 per person, meaning a program cost of ₹142 Crores in Andhra Pradesh.

In their original countries, both programs led to an estimated 55% reduction in domestic violence by the end of the intervention, and benefits that were estimated to last for at least another four years.

Annually, domestic violence among the targeted women leads to about 19 deaths in Andhra Pradesh. Either of these programs would avoid about 11 deaths annually, along with many medical injuries including eye injuries, bruises, dislocations, and broken bones.

This has spillover effects. Women who are victims of spousal abuse have to miss paid work, unpaid domestic work, and free time. Each assault on average costs a woman 5.5 days.

This reduction in productivity is a huge loss to the Andhra Pradesh economy. The cost to the entire formal and informal economy in 2018 from all married women is a whopping 1.8% of GSDP or ₹13,000 crore per year.

Helping just the 17 lakh women would create total benefits worth about four thousand crore, meaning that either of the two programs would have benefits worth somewhere in the region of 20 rupees for every rupee spent.

Expanding the cheaper program to the entire state of Andhra Pradesh would cost ₹1,500 crore but the benefits would increase to a phenomenal 28,000 crore.

Reducing domestic violence is not only morally imperative, but can help Andhra Pradesh become more productive and generate benefits worth many thousands of crores of rupees.

Interventions	BCR	Benefit	Cost
Self Help Group-based Intervention for combating Violence Against Women (SHGIVAW)	22	₹3073 crore	₹141.7 crore
Community Mobilisation-Based Intervention for Combating Violence Against Women (CMBIVAW)	19	₹3073 crore	₹163.5 crore

Total costs and benefits are discounted at 5%

Top Healthcare Priorities for Investment

The Indian healthcare sector has improved in both quality and quantity, enhancing the wellbeing of communities and the development of the nation. This is most evident in the dramatic increase in life expectancy: In 1901, the average Indian lived just 24 years. Even after independence, in 1951 life expectancy had climbed to a paltry 32 years. Today, the average Indian reaches 69 years of life, or more than what used to be two lifetimes.

This is because of a phenomenal decline in infant and maternal deaths, because major communicable diseases have been brought under control, and smallpox and polio have been eliminated.

However, the overall performance of the healthcare sector remains below international benchmarks. When it comes to strengthening the entire system, what should be the priorities for investment?

Looking at ways to strengthen the healthcare system, the first approach recommended by researchers PR Sodani, Neeraj Sharma, Md Mahbub Hossain, SD Gupta,, and DK Mangal of IIHMR University, Jaipur, is to improve the service quality of maternal health interventions. This requires a string of investments across the entire course of human birth, from ensuring family planning for the last few who still lack access, to ensuring that all mothers are provided with transportation and access to facility births or have skilled attendants at home births. It also involves improving availability of more high-tech equipment and personnel to tackle serious complications like obstructed labour, ante-partum and post-partum haemorrhage and eclampsia.

In Andhra Pradesh, the researchers find that ensuring all women have access to all or almost all of these interventions will over the next two decades cost about ₹3,000 crores. In total, this investment would save more than 6,000 mothers and 20,000 newborns· Put into financial terms, the total benefits to society would be worth ₹22,000 crores. In other words, each rupee spent on these maternal health interventions would generate benefits worth seven rupees.

Averted deaths per year from improved maternal health care

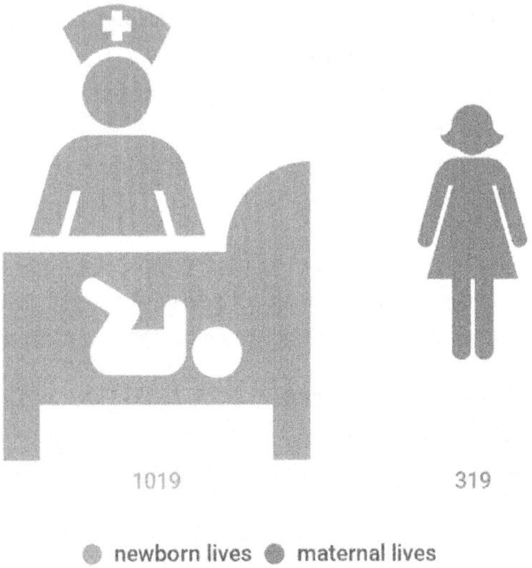

A shortage of ambulances means that people die due to delays in reaching timely healthcare facilities. Prior research suggests that there should be about 33 ambulances for every million people in urban areas, and three-times more in rural areas.

The new analysis shows some tough choices need to be made. Providing sufficient ambulances for the urban areas of Andhra Pradesh would over a decade cost about a thousand crore rupees. But it would save 4,236 lives each year among patients of Ischemic heart disease, road traffic accidents, and obstructed labour. Each rupee spent on strengthening ambulance services would generate social benefits worth a very worthy ₹17.

But the researchers' analysis shows that there is a huge difference in the efficiency of serving urban and rural areas. An adequate number of ambulances in rural Andhra Pradesh could save almost three times the number of lives each year. But unfortunately, the cost would skyrocket to 8-times the cost of urban ambulances. Each rupee invested would generate more modest social benefits worth ₹6. These are still considerable returns compared to many policy choices, but the stark difference highlights challenging decisions that policymakers will need to make.

Improved ambulance services 10-year costs and benefits

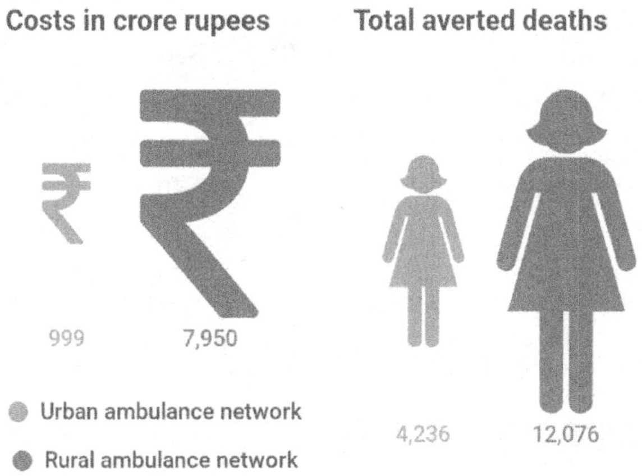

Finally, the researchers highlight the huge benefits from investment in family planning, to help women ensure space between pregnancies. Doing so has a huge range of benefits: it prevents unwanted pregnancy-related health risks in women, indirectly reduces infant mortality, reduces the spread of sexually transmitted diseases, empowers people and enhances education, reduces adolescent pregnancy, and helps in reducing population growth. Roughly five percent of the female population in the state still need contraceptives. Targeting these women is a challenge, but this can be achieved by expanding access to family planning services.

The total cost is ₹386 crores for Andhra Pradesh. Most benefits come from demographic dividends but also from child and maternal lives saved due to family planning methods would also be important. The total economic and social benefits would be worth about ₹6,310 crore for Andhra Pradesh. This means every rupee would generate societal benefits worth about 16-times the investment.

These quite remarkable returns highlight the impact that can be made by carefully focusing on further strengthening health systems, to close remaining gaps.

Interventions	BCR	Benefit	Cost
Improved urban 108 ambulance services (Time horizon 10 years)	17	₹16,837 crore	₹999 crore
Family planning for unmet need (annualised)	16	₹6,310 /capita	₹386 /capita
Strengthening basic and surgical capacity for reducing maternal and neonatal deaths (Time horizon 20 years)	7	₹22,107 crore	₹3,028 crore
Improved rural 108 ambulance services (Time horizon 10 years)	6	₹47,867 crore	₹7,950 crore

Total costs and benefits are discounted at 5%

Improving the Ease of Doing Business: Land Record Reform Will Open Doors for Business

While India climbed a phenomenal 30 spots to the 100th position out of 190 surveyed countries in the World Bank's 'ease of doing business' index this year, investors have ample choice among Indian states.

Investor perception is key, and each state wants to make sure that it is competitive. New research findings identify specific policies that would help gain an advantage.

Nirupama Soundararajan and Shagun Khurana from Pahle India Foundation have looked at how business reforms can help Andhra Pradesh get ahead.

Andhra Pradesh scored 99.73% on the Department of Industrial Policy & Promotion's ease-of-doing-business ranking. The researchers argue that Andhra Pradesh can make progress by further easing the process of land acquisition. Andhra Pradesh has made it relatively easy to obtain land – something that is generally true of states with a high number of industrial parks.

The researchers suggest that to streamline the land market further, the state government needs to move towards a conclusive land titling system. All records related to land – including record of rights, maps, and surveys – need to be digitised.

So far, the state revenue department has completed survey activities under the Digital India Land Records Modernisation Programme (DILRMP) for just 131 villages (0.75 per cent). It has digitized 57 per cent of existing maps (but has not updated any); all existing cadastral maps were prepared using traditional techniques.

Because it lags behind in digitisation, Andhra Pradesh has an opportunity to start from scratch and do things properly. Ensuring clear property titles can go a long way in making the land market more transparent and efficient.

Completion of survey and re-survey activities and digitisation of cadastral maps will have a total cost of about ₹213 crores. However, this will have multiple benefits. Evidence shows that strengthening property rights reduces the risk of expropriation and corruption. It also improves the mechanisms for peaceful resolution of disputes and contract enforcement. Perhaps most importantly, as land is more securely owned, it will be more advantageous for investors to spend money making land more productive, because owners are more likely to reap the benefits. This will all drive economic growth.

Based on a raft of studies across the world showing how more secure property rights drive the economy, the researchers calculate this would mean a 0.024 percentage point boost to the growth rate of the economy of Andhra Pradesh – which may sound slight, but would equate to ₹10,900 crores, or benefits that are worth 51-times the costs.

Ensuring that investors can buy and sell land with confidence is a winner.

Interventions	BCR	Benefit	Cost
Land record management system, conducting survey and re-survey activities, and digitise cadastral maps	51	₹10,938.37 crore	₹213.41 crore

Total costs and benefits are discounted at 5%

Mother-and-Child Health: A Smart Opportunity to Transform Lives in Andhra Pradesh

Andhra Pradesh has improved significantly on its maternal and child survival indicators in the last decade: between 2005-06 and 2015-16, survey data indicate that Andhra Pradesh's infant mortality fell from 54 to 35 deaths per 1000 live births (NFHS 3, NFHS4), and the maternal mortality rate fell from 134 per 100,000 live births in 2008, to 92 in 2012 (Ministry of Health and Family Welfare, NFHS-4, with data for undivided Andhra Pradesh).

Nevertheless, there is still room for improvement, particularly on several indicators related to access and use of child and maternal health services. Seventy percent of women exclusively breastfeed, 76 percent of women had at least four antenatal care visits during pregnancy, and 65 percent of children are fully vaccinated (NFHS-4).

Abusaleh Shariff, Chief Scholar of the US-India Policy Institute, looks at this situation.

Andhra Pradesh has made considerable improvements in mother and child health, with 76 percent of pregnant mothers now making at least four antenatal clinic visits. The programme Mana Bhavita (started as Maarpu) aims to bring a quick decline in infant and maternal mortality rates and malnutrition, while the Talli-Bidda Express scheme focuses on providing safe and hygienic transportation from government facilities to homes for new mothers, babies, and pregnant mothers who go for routine ANC visits.

The first intervention Dr Shariff suggests is providing an incentive to each mother of ₹2000, expanding the present-day system. The total cost for Andhra Pradesh is ₹163 crores, with the bulk being cash incentives. (The remainder is increased costs to the health system and private costs to mothers). This could reduce neonatal mortality by 6 per 1000 live births, based on similar programs, saving 804 infant lives in Andhra Pradesh annually.

The new research uses cost-benefit analysis, which puts benefits—including health, social, environmental and economic benefits—into numbers, so policies can be compared. In this case, Dr Shariff estimates the benefits are ₹950 crores annually. Every rupee achieves six rupees of benefits to society, which is a good return on investment.

Cash incentive for ANC visits cost breakdown

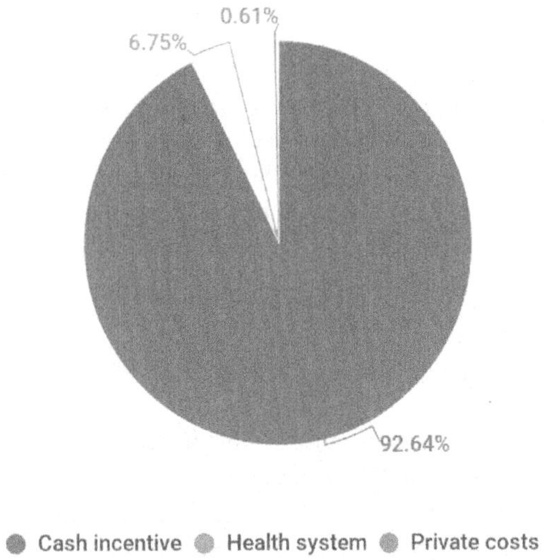

The researcher also studies a breastfeeding mass media campaign, using television advertisements and counselling. In Andhra Pradesh, 70 percent of mothers exclusively breastfeed. Based on international evidence, a campaign could increase this to 93 percent, saving nearly 6,000 lives. The policy would have benefits to Andhra Pradesh worth around 8-times the costs.

By far the most compelling case in the new research paper is for expanding immunisation programs in lagging districts. Just 65 percent of children in Andhra Pradesh are fully vaccinated, so there is a gap to close. Additionally, several districts lag behind the state average in terms of percentage of full immunization (East Godavari, Sri PottiSriramulu Nellore, Srikakulam and Vizianagaram). The average rate of immunization in these districts is 55%. This intervention targets these districts where 2.2 lakh children are born every year.

Promotion of breastfeeding, cost breakdown

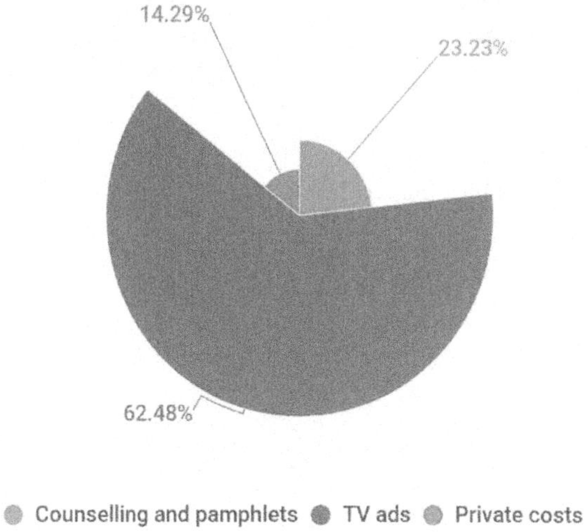

Based on a trial in Rajasthan, Dr Shariff proposes setting up 'immunization camps' in the lagging districts, providing lentils and meals worth ₹685 to parents for vaccinating their children. The policy would cost ₹10 crores in Andhra Pradesh and, if it raised the level of fully immunized children to the state average, would save 219 children annually.

Immunization would generate benefits worth more than ₹30 for every rupee spent, which is a considerable return on investment.

New data on costs and benefits closes evidence gaps and helps ensure more good can be done with each rupee. Focusing on interventions to further improve mother and child health would help save lives and strongly enhance the overall wellbeing of Andhra Pradesh.

Interventions	BCR	Benefit	Cost
Breastfeeding mass media promotion and intensive counselling (annual)	8	₹5,757 crore	₹749 crore
Immunization promotion, incentivization and supply in lagging districts (annual)	37	₹385 crore	₹10 crore
Conditional cash transfer for ANC visits (annual)	6	₹950 crore	₹163 crore

Total costs and benefits are discounted at 5%

Non-Communicable Diseases: Huge Payoffs from Focus on Diabetes and Heart Disease

India's rapid growth means infectious diseases are increasingly being vanquished. Yet, as more people live longer lives, this is somewhat counterbalanced by an increase in the toll of chronic disease – what the health community calls non-communicable diseases (NCDs). According to the Global Burden of Disease, 54% of all Indian deaths in 1990 were due to communicable diseases (along with maternal, neonatal and nutritional diseases), whereas just 38% came from NCDs (the last 8% were caused by injuries). But since 2001, NCDs have claimed more lives. By 2016 they caused 62% of all deaths. This will only keep increasing, with one estimate showing NCDs and mental health conditions will cost India an astonishing $4.58 trillion between 2012 and 2030 – about twice the *total* GDP of India today.

Recognizing this shift, the Government launched the National Program for Prevention and Control of Cancer, Diabetes, CVD and Stroke (NPCDCS) in 2011. Most states have initiated activities with technical and financial support from the central government. However, much more needs to be done, since there are many more lives that can be saved.

Professor Shreelata Rao Seshadri of Azim Premji University, with co-author Vijayalakshmi Hebbare, show that policy-makers can achieve a lot by prioritizing particular strategies against specific NCDs.

Take diabetes. It will cost India ₹9.7 trillion (USD$150 billion) between 2012 and 2030. In Andhra Pradesh, about 1-in-3 people are deemed overweight or obese, and one-in-ten have high or very high blood sugar—much higher rates than the national average.

On current trends, diabetes will claim the lives of 159,000 AP adults aged 30-69 in 2030. Reaching half with screening and treatment with Metformin therapy, with realistic coverage and adherence rates, will cost around ₹2,000 per person annually, or about ₹590 crore over the next 13 years. This would save more than 11,000 lives annually and reduce chronic suffering by more than 10%. The benefits from avoided death and disease would reach more than 18-times the cost.

The evidence is even more compelling for combating cardiovascular disease (CVD), which is a leading killer in India. By itself, it will cost 130 trillion rupees between 2012 and 2030 – almost the equivalent of eradicating one year of India's entire GDP. In AP, among 30-69 year-olds, nearly one lakh people will die this year from cardiovascular disease.

The answer is relatively simple: a screening program to identify those at high risk, and putting those with elevated blood pressure on a cheap "polypill". This could effectively avoid more than 2.6 lakh deaths over the next 13 years, at an average cost of about ₹4,000 per treated person. The total cost of ₹4,400 crore will result in benefits (meaning less death and disease) worth 31-times the costs.

However, some NCDs don't present such simple solutions. The authors look at cervical cancer and breast cancer, both serious problems that need tackling. Unfortunately, screening costs are around the same level as those to tackle CVD, yet the benefits are much lower. Cervical cancer kills about 1,800 women each year in AP, but even an ambitious screening and treatment program costing ₹3,200 crore would save just 600 lives, meaning the return on each rupee is just 1.6 rupees in social benefits. Breast cancer screening would be even costlier, saving just tens of lives annually.

India's development will make NCDs the next great health challenge, but not all investments are equally effective. The evidence shows that adequate coverage of screening and treatment services at the primary level for diabetes and especially for heart disease can avert a large number of deaths in a very cost-effective manner. These arguments should make such programs very attractive for politicians in Andhra Pradesh.

Comparison of costs and averted deaths

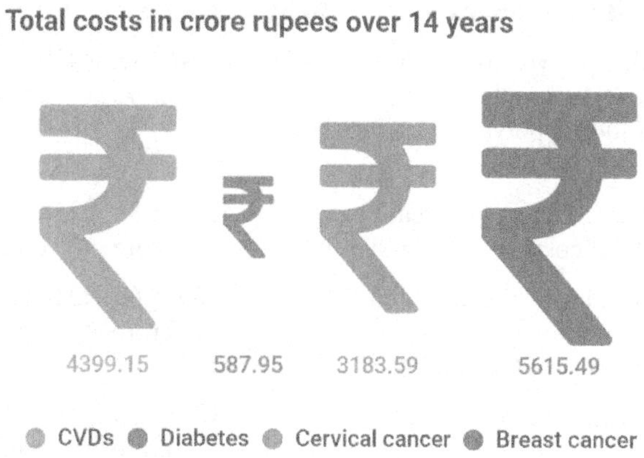

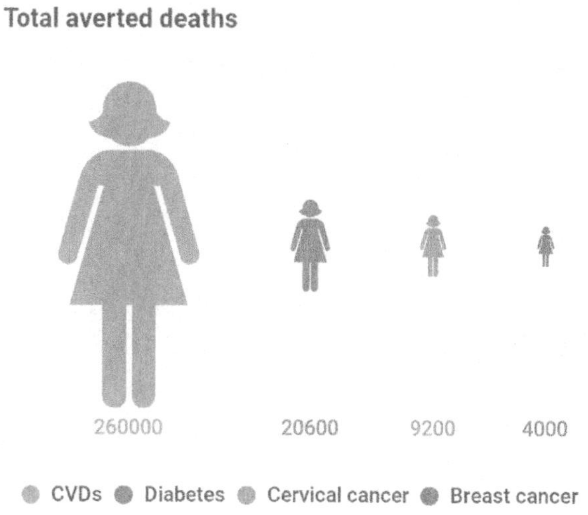

Interventions	BCR	Benefit	Cost
Secondary prevention of cardiovascular disease through use of a multidrug polypill (total costs for 14 years)	31	₹136464.13 crore	₹4399.15 crore
Diabetes screening and treatment (total costs for 14 years)	18	₹10723.39 crore	₹587.95 crore
Cervical cancer screening and treatment (total costs for 14 years)	1.6	₹5038.69 crore	₹3183.59 crore
Breast cancer screening and treatment (total costs for 14 years)	0.4	₹2165.55 crore	₹5615.49 crore

Total costs and benefits are discounted at 5%

NUTRITION: A DEVELOPMENT INVESTMENT FOR THE AGES

Proper early nutrition can spectacularly change the entire life trajectory of a child. We know from long-term studies that it promotes brain development, making the child do better in school, and much better later in life, affecting everything from the happiness of marriages to the quality of jobs, and up to 60% more earnings.

India has made significant progress in reducing child malnutrition, but with nearly half of all deaths of children aged under-five mainly caused by poor diet, much still needs to be done. Where could new policies make the biggest impact?

Proportion of underweight children below 5 years

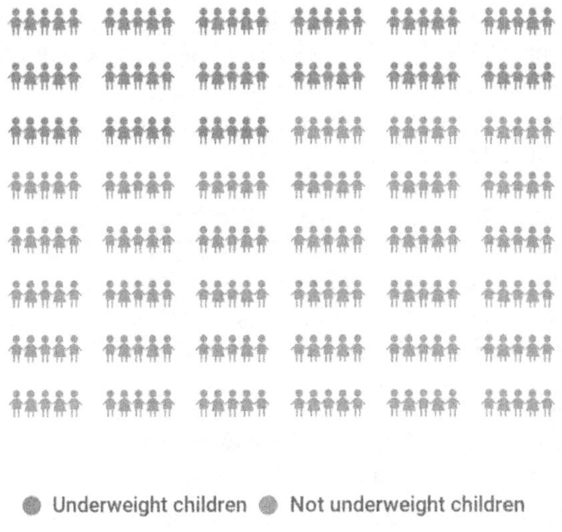

William Joe and Abhishek Kumar of Institute of Economic Growth, and S.V. Subramanian of Harvard T. H. Chan School of Public Health, have undertaken analysis on how Andhra

Pradesh could reach more young children and pregnant and lactating mothers.

In Andhra Pradesh, where 60% of reproductive-age women are anaemic and a high percentage of children under five are stunted, the progress of nutrition programs has been slow, and the potential from investment in nutrition is great.

Direct nutrition-based interventions include counselling for behaviour change, supplementary food and micronutrient supplements, which are primarily delivered through the government health programmes. A 10 percent increase in coverage would avoid 181 deaths, and reduce stunting by 20% in the population receiving the intervention. Each rupee spent will be worth 9 rupees in benefits.

The health status of a child is inextricably linked to the health status of the mother. Women who are anaemic are likely to deliver low birth weight babies, who are likely to remain anaemic and suffer from cumulative growth and development deficit. Adequate nutritional health is critical for safe motherhood and to break the otherwise perpetual intergenerational cycle of undernutrition. In India, there is very high prevalence of both maternal and child undernutrition.

All children below 6 years of age, pregnant women and lactating mothers are eligible for availing of supplementary food services under the Integrated Child Development Scheme (ICDS) which is funded by both Central and State government. Supplementary nutrition need to be better targeted towards those sections that actually require the appropriate nutrition.

The primary beneficiaries are children aged 6-12 and 12-36 months and pregnant and lactating women. The benefits will accrue through reduction in deaths and morbidity from specific diseases due to provision of improved nutrition. It is estimated that 161 lives will be saved for a ten percent increase in coverage. Stunting will be reduced by 18% in the population receiving the intervention. Benefits realized per beneficiary are ₹107,135, 89 per cent of which represent improved lifetime productivity from avoided stunting. At a cost of 10,341 rupees per beneficiary, each rupee spent will achieve 10 rupees worth of social good.

Another intervention the researchers look at is micronutrient supplementation for pregnant women during ANC visits. The focus is on providing Vitamin A supplementation, iron, iodine, calcium, zinc and ORS. At a total cost of 88 crore rupees for one year, this intervention can avoid 106,882 cases of maternal anaemia, 25,293 low birth weight babies, 113 maternal deaths, 19,103 preterm births, 1,337 preterm deaths and 210 stillbirths in Andhra Pradesh. Each rupee spent targeting supplements to pregnant women in antenatal care would have benefits worth nearly 40 rupees.

Yearly impact of micronutrient supplements for pregnant women during ANC visits

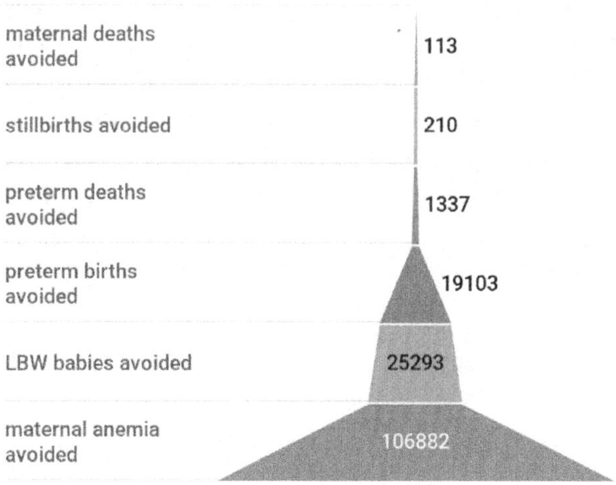

The researchers also look at interpersonal counselling for behaviour change. Diarrhoea is a major cause of deaths among children under 5 years of age in Andhra Pradesh. Low socioeconomic status, poor maternal literacy, inadequate breastfeeding, malnutrition, poor sanitation and hygiene practices of the mother or the caretaker are the major determinants of diarrheal diseases.

A six-year intervention which includes counselling for breastfeeding and counselling for complementary feeding and hand washing will help to avoid 240 deaths in Andhra Pradesh which are related to diarrhoea. Every rupee spent will yield more than 60 rupees in benefits to society.

Seldom in life are the benefits of simple, cheap policies so obvious and clear-cut: the new evidence points unambiguously to massive benefits from prioritizing closing gaps in access to nutrition interventions.

Interventions	BCR	Benefit	Cost
Education of mothers for breastfeeding, complementary feeding and hand-washing	61	₹71,423 /mother	₹1,177 /mother
Micronutrients for pregnant women at ANC visits	39	₹34,678 /mother	₹884 /mother
Supplementary food for mother and child	10	₹107,135 /beneficiary	₹10,341 /beneficiary
Package of nutrition based interventions	9	₹120,824 /beneficiary	₹12,885 /beneficiary
Community based treatment of children with severe acute malnutrition (SAM) using ready-to-use therapeutic food (RUTF)	4	₹32,523 /child	₹8,829 /child

Total costs and benefits are discounted at 5%

POVERTY: EVALUATING THE CHOICES TO HELP

In recent times, microcredit schemes have been presented as a panacea, attracting billions of rupees around the world. However, a series of trials have now shown that microcredit doesn't do much good – often not even increasing average incomes, and schemes can bury the poor in debt.

Subsidized crop insurance is another direct approach designed to help generate more income for the poorest of farmers by making agriculture less risky. But how useful is this approach? Munshi Sulaiman, Research Director of Save the Children International with Michael Murigi of the University of Sydney, analytically weigh up the costs and benefits of this along with other direct approaches to poverty.

Pradhan Mantri Fasal Bima Yojana (PMFBY) is the most recent—and most comprehensive—crop insurance model, launched in 2016 and reaching some 39 million farmers. Typically, the insurance premium is almost entirely paid by the central and state governments. In Andhra Pradesh as an example, the researchers find that PMFBY, if expanded from 22% coverage today to 50% coverage in 2024, will cost around two lakh crore rupees.

This expenditure generates a number of benefits, including the actual insurance pay-outs, and allows farmers to take higher risks on more valuable crops that rely on bigger levels of rainfall. The insurance safety net means fewer suicides and less malnutrition for farming families.

While protecting farmers from income shocks is an important outcome on its own, the benefit of insurance coverage on farmers risk taking behaviour, investment decisions and impact on productivity are the major economic justification for subsidizing crop insurance.

In the long run, two-thirds of the benefits come from the pay-out and one-quarter from higher profits. In total, every rupee spent on the policy achieves societal good worth about ₹1.40 rupees in Andhra Pradesh.

In this case, the direct approach to alleviating poverty by subsidizing insurance does achieve more than it costs, but it can hardly be said that it has dramatic returns.

Another approach is a direct response to poverty that combines very specific interventions in a way that has been shown to have an immediate and sustained impact on food consumption, income, savings as well as assets.

Eliminating extreme poverty depends critically on creating sustainable livelihoods for the economically active ultra-poor: households who are landless and primarily rely on casual work for their livelihoods. The success of a "Graduation Approach" in a number of countries has made it a critical tool in social protection schemes. More than forty countries are now implementing different versions of this model, at various scales.

This approach was forged by the world's largest non-governmental organization (NGO), BRAC, and is implemented at small scale by various NGOs in West Bengal, Andhra Pradesh, and Jharkhand.

This model follows a strict set of targeting criteria to reach the ultra-poor and provides time-bound support that usually lasts between 18 and 24 months. First, food or money is given to the poor to ease the stress of daily survival; second, beneficiaries are encouraged to start savings. Third, they are provided with livestock or other income-generating assets. Following this, there is training provided in both technical skills and life skills. Finally, beneficiaries are provided with health support.

Each intervention costs more than ₹25,000, with half of this spent on the asset and food. Reaching 30% of poor households would cost ₹11.2 billion in Andhra Pradesh. Based on long-term studies from West Bengal, the increase in annual household consumption, savings and assets will mean every rupee spent will achieve at least ₹3.50 of social benefits and possibly even ₹5 – making it two- to three-times more effective as farmer insurance subsidies.

Cost-benefit ratio assuming different time horizon of the consumption effects of poverty graduation programs

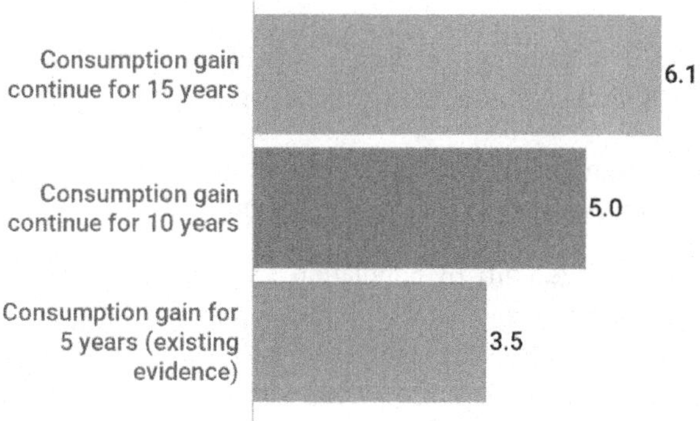

Interventions	BCR	Benefit	Cost
Ultra-poor graduation including asset transfer, health services and coaching (for 30% of all poor households)	3.5	₹3,955 crore	₹1,117 crore
Subsidised crop insurance until 2032	1.4	₹28,806 crore	₹21,189 crore

Total costs and benefits are discounted at 5%

How Green Transport Solutions Could Transform Vijayawada

Vijayawada is booming. The local economy is expected to reach ₹1,156 billion by 2025, a six-fold increase over 2010.

Rapid economic growth means more commerce and more people, which means more traffic and congestion.

India's 43rd biggest city by population, by some measures is the third-most densely populated city *in the world.* Clogged roads not only make life frustrating, but also slow economic progress: they prevent burgeoning businesses and cities from reaching their full potential.

Between FY16 and FY17, the number of motorbikes and cars increased by 73 per cent and 40 per cent respectively. Air pollution levels have increased too, and are now nearly double the national average.

This all means that, like many other Indian cities, major challenges include growth in the number of private vehicles, traffic congestion and mounting city pollution. There is only a limited public transport system due to the high costs of land and reluctance of the public to part with land. This means that widening of roads to accommodate a mass transit system at road level is very difficult.

Parijat Dey, Senior Manager of IL&FS, and Ankush Malhotra, Vice President, UMTC, look at two ways of resolving these problems.

The researchers examine two options to bring down the low-capacity, private share in passenger traffic to 20 percent by 2052: a metro with a feeder network, and a dedicated bus corridor with electric public transport.

Either option would likely require funding from Central or State government or from international agencies such as the Asia Development Bank, World Bank, or others.

The first approach would involve the development of two elevated metro corridors with 25 stations, stretching 26 km, to cater to half of the city's population by 2052. This would also include more bus services and intermediate public transport (IPT). Further, considering the population growth of the city, a medium capacity metro system with capacity for about 30,000-45,000 passengers traveling per hour per direction of traffic would help to serve the future needs of the city.

The metro's capital expenditure, worth ₹64 billion, is the most expensive single cost, with capital expenditure for the metro feeder and IPT coming to roughly half that. There's also a significant social cost of disruption due to the construction, which the researchers estimate would come to about ₹50 billion. In total, the costs would amount to some ₹200 billion.

Metro and feeder busses yearly costs and benefits in crore ₹

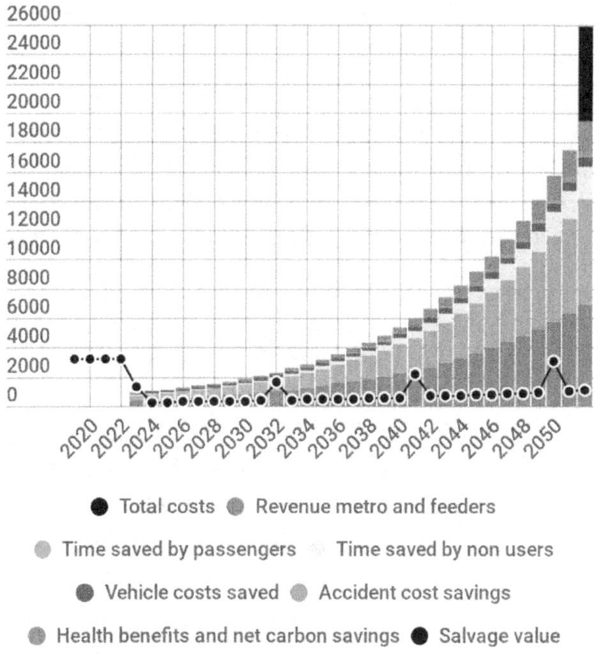

Benefits would be sizeable. The city would make ₹320 billion or so in revenue, and passengers would save a considerable amount of time, worth some ₹200 billion.

There are environmental benefits from less carbon being emitted, fuel costs, reductions in traffic accidents, and health benefits from the cut in air pollution. Added together, these come to ₹661 billion. This means that each rupee spent would generate benefits to society worth more than 3 rupees.

In the second approach, two elevated bus rapid transport corridors would be constructed, the same length as the proposed metro route, to cater 50 percent of the city population by 2052. Additionally, bus services and intermediate public transport would be increased, to the benchmark set by Ministry of Housing and Urban Affairs for urban transport for Indian cities.

Capital expenditure costs amount to about half of the total costs of ₹164 billion. The disruption cost would be lower than the first option, at around ₹14 billion.

Benefits are nearly as vast as for the metro. Revenue would account for nearly half of all benefits, at about ₹323 billion; time savings by passengers would be worth another ₹200 billion; and reductions in health costs would add up to about ₹41 billion. This all adds up to ₹664 billion, meaning each rupee generates benefits worth 4 rupees.

These analyses show the way for Vijayawada and other cities to prepare for growth and expansion, and ensure that today's traffic, pollution and accident problems do not become tomorrow's chokehold on development.

Interventions	BCR	Benefit	Cost
Elevated Bus Rapid Transit (BRT)	4.0	₹66,380 crore	₹16,462 crore
Metro with feeder buss network	3.3	₹66,179 crore	₹20,148 crore

Total costs and benefits are discounted at 5%

Upskilling India: Which Policies Should Get Priority?

When India found itself in 103rd position in the recent World Economic Forum ranking of 130 nations on the preparedness of talent, it was just another indication of the skills challenge. In just five years, the Government's Skill Gap Analysis Report estimates that an extra 40 crore workers need to be skilled, reskilled or up-skilled. The current official estimate is that slightly more than half a crore people are being trained annually.

Mansi Arora, Rajesh Chakrabarti, and Kushal Sagar Prakash from Sunay Policy Advisory have undertaken an analysis of three skills policies.

In Andhra Pradesh, the skills challenge is clear: more than 97 per-cent of the 21 lakh individuals expected to join the workforce between now and 2022 will be totally or partially unskilled according to the National Skills Development Corporation. To meet demand, Andhra Pradesh needs to skill about half of its workforce entering the labour market by 2022, or 10.5 lakh people

Andhra Pradesh has undertaken an integrated skilling initiative, and the AP State Skill Development Corporation (APSSDC) has been established as a public-private partnership, with the hope of skilling two crore people in 15 years.

The new research can help policy-makers by focusing on one important question: what is achieved with each additional rupee spent by AP on each skills policy?

The first policy examined is the provision of loan assistance to small and medium enterprises (SMEs) to encourage expansion and job creation. This may seem a roundabout route to up-skilling, but as a powerhouse of SMEs (like many Indian states), Andhra Pradesh can create jobs by supporting their growth and development\.

Research suggests that every rupee of loan will increase SME profit by about 0.89 rupees. Factoring borrowing costs, administration fees and default rates, it costs 16 rupees for every 100 rupees loaned. The researchers conclude that each rupee would generate benefits to the economy worth 5.6 rupees – a solid return on investment.

But to compete on a global stage, Andhra Pradesh needs direct upskilling policies. One approach studied is apprenticeship schemes that combine vocational education with work-based learning. For the employer, the cost is ₹1.5 lakh, including salary, supervision, training, and administration. The government spends another ₹0.2 lakh reimbursing employers, and on marketing. The individual misses out on about ₹0.16 lakh in income during the apprenticeship. The total cost to everyone involved for one apprenticeship is approximately ₹1.9 lakh.

The employee receives a substantial income increase over their working life, worth about ₹11.2 lakh. The employer benefits to the tune of ₹2.2 lakh, by having a more productive and job-ready workforce, increased revenue, and savings from having to recruit. Total benefits are ₹13.4 Lakh. Every rupee, therefore, spent on a year-long apprenticeship program is worth 7.2 rupees to the Andhra Pradesh economy. This is even stronger than supporting SMEs in generating societal benefits.

Finally, the authors look at expanding the current vocational training program to incentivize more people to join. This is job-specific, technical and hands-on. A similar analysis is undertaken: this time, the cost for each apprenticeship, both public and private, is about ₹0.46 lakh.

The results are marked: an individual will earn ₹7.2 lakh more over their lifetime. (This accounts for expected income growth as well as changing workforce participation and unemployment). The analysis reveals that benefits to society are 16-times higher than the costs. Spending one rupee to generate 16 rupees in benefits to society is a very compelling investment.

Cost breakdown of training program vs. apprenticeship

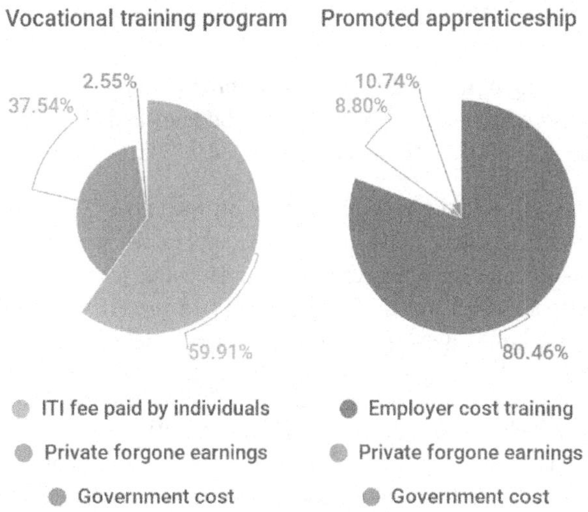

This research highlights the strong case for Andhra Pradesh to invest more in expanding access vocational training programs – and the need to study the costs and benefits of skills policy options across India.

Interventions	BCR	Benefit	Cost
Vocational training	16	₹716,403 /individual	₹43,818 /individual
Apprenticeship	7	₹1,337,490 /individual	₹186,218 /individual
Credit support to MSME	6	89% of credit	16% of credit

Total costs and benefits are discounted at 5%

Social Housing: The Best Ways to Help the Poor

On assuming power in 2014, the Government set out to improve housing conditions for the urban poor, and launched Housing for All (HFA) by 2022 - 'Pradhan Mantri Awas Yojana Urban'.

New analysis examines the efficiency of three possible paths to achieve this goal. It shows that some approaches are stronger than others, and the result can help the Housing and Urban Affairs Department to re-think the delivery of the HFA by 2022 agenda for large cities. It also prompts the broader question as to whether non-housing policies might better help the urban poor.

The comprehensive report on costs and benefits from housing policies is written by Amitabh Kundu, Distinguished Fellow at the Research and Information System for Developing Countries and Arjun Kumar, Visiting Fellow at the Institute for Human Development.

The first approach examined is Beneficiary-led Construction (BLC), where households with land or a house can claim a subsidy of ₹1.5 lakh for construction or an extension. This initiative is effectively driven by the beneficiaries. Costs include land and construction, and managing and supervising the construction. The benefits are many – like better living quarters, better health and better opportunity for a family to live together. All of these – and more – benefits are explicitly priced through the increased market value of the property.

In large cities in Andhra Pradesh, the total cost of building a 300 sq. feet house is estimated under this scheme at ₹10 lakh, while Drs Kundu and Kumar find that the benefit – the increased market price – works out at nearly ₹13 lakh. Each rupee creates benefits worth a little more than one rupee.

The second approach is the Affordable Housing in Partnership (AHP) scheme, where projects are undertaken by public and private sectors in partnership, and 35 percent of houses are to be reserved for the economically weaker. This is a "supply-side" intervention to be led by private developers. The total cost of constructing a 300 sq. feet house under AHP in large cities in Andhra Pradesh is estimated at about ₹7 lakh, with construction accounting for more than half. In addition to the market price rise, there is also a profit gained by the builder, which should be considered as part of the benefits to society, but given less weight because the builder will be in a different income group than poor beneficiaries.

The new analysis shows that total benefits to society come to nearly ₹12 lakh, so this achieves more than BLC, at nearly two rupees for each rupee spent.

The final approach examined by Drs Kundu and Kumar is In-situ Slum Redevelopment (ISSR), which leverages the land currently locked by slums, and involves re-housing slum dwellers in better accommodation in the same place, with the participation of private developers. This has no land cost, as the land is effectively already occupied. Consequently, the only costs are those of construction; internal and external infrastructure; community mobilization; project management; and providing transit accommodation.

Under this approach, the cost of a 300 sq. feet house in a large city in Andhra Pradesh comes to just over ₹4 lakh. In addition to the market price rise, slum dwellers get additional benefits, including a reduction in death and healthcare spending, along with time savings because of access to basic amenities, especially water and sanitation.

Taking this into account, the approach generates benefits worth nearly ₹11 lakh, so each rupee achieves about two-and-a-half rupees in benefits.

₹ lakh costs and benefits per 300 sq. feet house

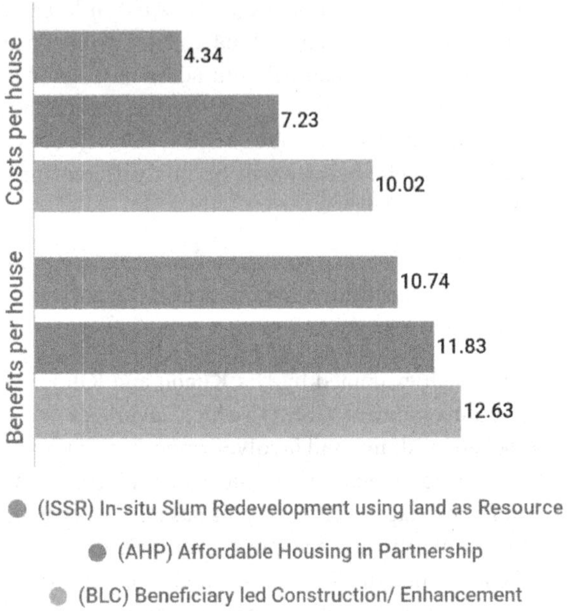

What are the lessons? For the Housing and Urban Affairs Department, it seems clear that among social housing approaches, ISSR should be top priority to achieve the most.

But there is perhaps a broader lesson, too. Other papers for *India Consensus* find policies helping the urban poor—such as investment in improved Tuberculosis screening and treatment, or improved water and sanitation access—that generate many, many-times more rupees of benefits, for every rupee spent.

Having a safe, secure home provides dignity and protection against life shocks, and is a noble, important goal for government to deliver; but if the goal is to help the urban poor as effectively as possible, governments should consider all of the data, including this economic evidence.

Interventions	BCR	Benefit	Cost
In-situ Slum Redevelopment using land as Resource (ISSR)	2.5	₹10.74 lakhs per house	₹4.34 lakhs per house
Affordable Housing in Partnership (AHP)	1.6	₹11.83 lakhs per house	₹7.23 lakhs per house
Beneficiary led Construction/ Enhancement (BLC)	1.3	₹12.63 lakhs per house	₹10.02 lakhs per house

Total costs and benefits are estimated for a 300 square feet house and discounted at 5%

LIFTING AP'S HEALTH RANKING AND SAVING THOUSANDS OF LIVES EVERY YEAR

The health status of Andhra Pradesh is gradually improving. In a recent ranking exercise on health indicators by NITI Aayog, it moved up one ranking among the 21 larger states for its performance in 2015-2016, to eight place from ninth.

However, when it came to tuberculosis (TB), one of the key measures on which states are judged, AP didn't do so well. The state saw the most significant decrease in the success rate of treating new confirmed cases, from 90.4% in 2014 to 88.5% in 2015, as compared to the other larger states.

For Andhra Pradesh and for every state, managing TB is especially important because in addition to claiming many lives, it has a cascading effect, since one case treated saves others from being infected. Managing this killer disease and especially the costly and increasing multi-drug resistant variant will mean the health system will have more money to tackle other health priorities.

AP is managing to identify more cases: the total case notification rate of TB per 100,000 people increased from 136 in 2015 to 145 in 2016. The national strategic plan for TB elimination, launched in 2017, set out a renewed ambition to control and eradicate the disease. The crucial question is how to make this happen.

Nimalan Arinaminpathy, a senior lecturer in Mathematical Epidemiology at the School of Public Health, Imperial College London, has explored two options that would improve the response to TB, and thus lift AP's health performance.

Dr Arinaminpathy's first proposal is to increase the quality of TB care in the private sector, by creating a 'Public Private Support Agency' (PPSA), also mentioned as one of the critical components in the NSP 2017-25 (National Strategic Plan). Mumbai and Patna have already engaged such agencies to identify and enlist private providers for case notification and follow up, supported by public funds and overseen by the national TB programme.

The Government of Andhra Pradesh has also started engaging with private sector health providers for TB care and control. About 13% of TB patients notified are from private sector.

Lifting the standard of TB care in the private sector is critical, since the National Strategic Plan (NSP) 2017-25 identifies that well over half of TB infected first go to private clinics. Poor compliance with patient management strategies and use of inaccurate tests can delay diagnosis, thus permitting ongoing transmission, while a general lack of treatment support means that many private patients do not complete the 6-month standard TB regimen. This leads to poorer outcomes than in the public sector, and increases the risk of multi-drug-resistance.

Importantly, unlike earlier public-private mix approaches, private providers would continue to manage TB patients. This is crucial to engage the private providers, so they don't just see the purpose of the PPSA to 'divert' the patient to the public sector.

To estimate the cost, Dr Arinaminpathy uses pilot study costs. He conservatively estimates that it will only manage to reach half of TB patients. In this scenario, the cost would be Rs 0.3 crore per year between now and 2050. This would increase the number of TB patients undergoing high-quality treatment by 2040 from 27.3 thousand to 32.9 thousand. This would save 2,264 lives every year on average, or 7.6% of the deaths that might otherwise have occurred.

To enable comparison of this policy with other interventions, Dr Arinaminpathy uses cost-benefit analysis to put into monetary terms the benefits of saving lives and reducing disability and treatment times. He finds that every rupee would generate 113 rupees of benefits. That's a remarkable 'return on investment'.

The second intervention adds improved case-finding. Currently, TB services largely wait for symptomatic patients to show up to a clinic. Case-finding aims to go into the community to detect TB cases. This would diagnose patients earlier, shorten the period over which they are infectious, and reach under-served populations. As in the NSP 2017-25, the research sets urban slums as a priority area: they have just 10% of the population but account for one-quarter of the TB burden. This is crucial for cities like Vishakapatnam and Vijayawada which have a high proportion of urban slums – around 40 % according to the 2011 census.

In these areas, under the proposal screening would be conducted once per year for TB using X-rays. Possible cases would be diagnosed using accurate, rapid tests. If positive, people would be referred to the public sector for treatment. This intervention would be supported, staffed and implemented by the national TB programme.

Yearly costs and cost savings in ₹ crores from improving private sector TB care and increasing active case finding

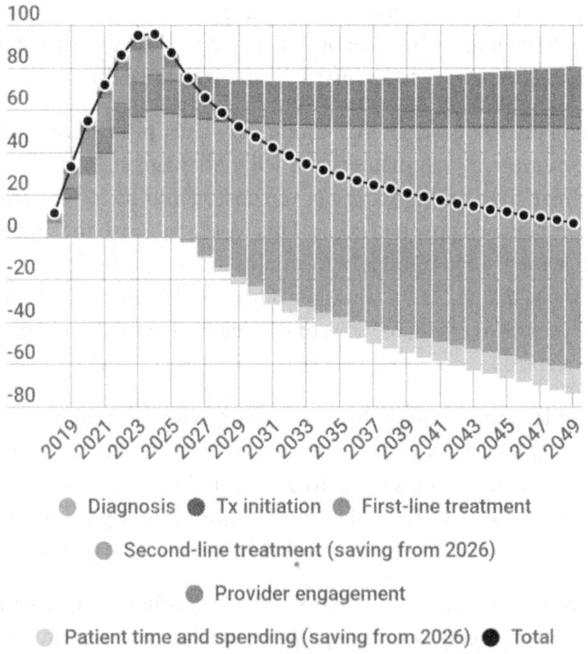

The analysis highlights two compelling approaches that could strongly boost AP's health performance, ensuring not only that thousands of lives are saved, but that resources are well-allocated so that the system runs better for all.

In combination with private sector engagement, the cost for the first years would be around ₹48.1 crores. Crucially, less TB will cut multi-drug resistant cases by up to 80%. Since these cases are much more expensive, it will mean much lower costs in later years, opening up opportunities for more spending on other health care challenges.

Case-finding would avert an average of 4,450 TB deaths per year, or 15% of deaths that might otherwise have occurred. The analysis shows that each rupee spent generates a return on investment worth 120 rupees.

Interventions	BCR	Benefit	Cost
Improve private sector TB care	117	₹51,598 crores	₹439.63 cores
Improve private sector TB care and implement active case finding	109	₹84,187 crores	₹775.96 crores

Total costs and benefits are discounted at 5%

Enhancing Andhra Pradesh's Trade Competitiveness

Free trade provides the greatest opportunity to improve human welfare, and has already helped lift more than a billion people out of poverty over the past quarter-century. India is transforming, thanks to its strong performance selling products and services around the globe.

But what interventions, at a state level, can do the most to ensure Indian exports are globally competitive?

Dr Amitendu Palit of the National University of Singapore provides answers.

The study using cost-benefit analysis looks at what policies would help the state improve even more—and reveals that some policies are much better than others. The researcher looks at approaches that would align with the ongoing coastal economic development strategy, Sagarmala, and with the state's strategy of coast-led industrial development which seeks to fully utilize the potential of having India's longest coastline.

One approach would be to upgrade one of Andhra Pradesh's ports with state-of-art facilities that significantly enhance its maritime trade capacity—and, at the same time, 'backward' linking of the port with the hinterland, to enable fast movement of cargo and a reduction in logistics costs.

The main costs include new and upgraded facilities – like a container freight station, expanded berths and more dredging, along with land acquisition and infrastructure like such as expanded highways. All these fixed costs are based on data from the recent Visakhapatnam Port modernisation. Including substantial operating costs over the 20 year period, the total cost comes to ₹1,985 crores.

The port capacity would increase by 20 million tonnes per annum, substantially increasing port revenue over the coming decades, totaling ₹1,695 crores. This amount is a lower bound estimate of the social benefit from this new port, but since it also partly cannibalizes other ports, it is likely that it reflects about the total social benefits for all of Andhra Pradesh. Thus, each rupee spent on a new state-of-the-art port would generate benefits worth slightly less than one rupee.

There can be strategic reasons for the government to focus on port development, but this rather slight return suggests that alternative trade enhancement policies deserve a higher priority for scarce resources.

Among other proposals is the development under Sagarmala of an export-oriented apparel park in a Coastal Economic Zone (CEZ) over 2000 acres dedicated primarily to exports. With implementation beginning in 2019, facilities for use by exporters would be expected to be completed by 2024. The total costs of land, development and operations would be vast, at ₹19,235 crores.

Yearly ₹ crore costs and CEZ export increase scenarios

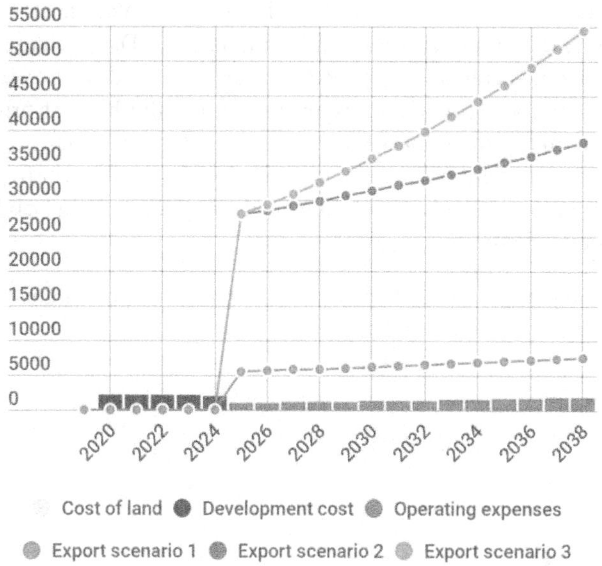

In addition to exports generated, there will be 'spillover' economic activity created, meaning the creation of new livelihoods, growth of ancillary industries, and urban and retail development in surrounding areas.

If the increased exports and spillover effects are as strong as has been seen in similar projects in China and other parts of Asia, the benefits could be in the region of 14-times the costs. However, based on the evidence from India's existing economic zones showing much more modest economic impact, each rupee would more likely achieve about 2.5 rupees of benefit.

The final proposal for Andhra Pradesh is designed to turbocharge marine exports, by establishing a laboratory equipped with the latest scientific testing facilities for certifying quality standard of seafood exports to the United States, European Union, Northeast Asia, Southeast Asia, and Middle East. Similar to the seafood certification facility at Vizag, this would encourage some seafood production currently targeting the domestic market to exports, including Vannamei shrimps.

A much cheaper initiative than the others explored, at ₹44 crores, the proposal has considerable returns. Driven largely by frozen shrimps, export revenues are expected to increase annually by two percent, as shrimps enjoy the highest price premium in global markets among all seafood exports. In total, the intervention is estimated to bring the social benefit of ₹346 crores, meaning each rupee achieves a significant eight rupees of benefits.

It is important that Indian states pick the best opportunities to continue to compete globally.

Interventions	BCR	Benefit	Cost
Scientific testing and certification facilities for marine product exports (Time horizon 10 years)	7.9	₹346 crore	₹44 crore
Development of an export-oriented Coastal Economic Zone (CEZ)			
Scenario 1 (Time horizon 20 years)	2.4	₹46,46 crore	₹19,235 crore
Scenario 2 (Time horizon 20 years)	12	₹237,726 crore	₹19,235 crore
Scenario 3 (Time horizon 20 years)	15	₹282,338 crore	₹19,235 crore
Modernizing port facilities and improving hinterland connectivity (Time horizon 10 years)	0.9	₹1,695 crore	₹1,985 crore

Total costs and benefits are discounted at 5%

Urban Growth: How Vijayawada Can Keep Pace with Infrastructure Needs

Cities are, in many ways, the future of India. The number of metropolitan cities with a population higher than 1 million jumped from 35 in 2001 to 50 in 2011, and is expected to reach 87 by 2031. Today, 40 crore people call an Indian metropolis home; that will double by 2050.

This swift growth places huge pressure on infrastructure that in very few cases was ever designed with so many people in mind. A major report in 2010 found that the duration of water supply in Indian cities ranges from 1-6 hours; only about 21 percent of waste water generated is treated; and less than one-third of municipal solid waste is segregated.

Parijat Dey of IL&FS and O Rajesh Babu from APUIAML look at opportunities to improve urban infrastructure in Vijayawada, Andhra Pradesh.

The researchers first look at the costs and benefits of providing 100% sewerage and wastewater treatment to the major city. In Vijayawada, just 36% of households have access to sewerage connections, and 35% of the sewage generated by the city is treated. Ensuring 100% coverage and provisions for wastewater treatment would cost ₹3,385 crore, with most being operating expenditure. The health benefits would be worth a large part of the ₹3,385 crore of benefits.

Greater returns would come, for every rupee spent, by focusing on solid waste management.

There is very little waste processing and treatment in Vijayawada. Past initiatives for waste processing have not been sustained. Segregation of waste at a household level is low.

Achieving 100% collection, transportation, and management with minimal amounts going to the landfill would cost around ₹1,300 crore, including both capital expenditure and operating spending.

There would be considerable benefits. Many of these can be identified by working out what citizens would pay to have improved solid waste management. There are also improvements in land value, and money gained from selling compost and Refuse derived fuel. In total, these benefits would be worth ₹2,800 crore to Vijayawada, including land value savings and revenue through sale of compost and RDF.

Showing a better return on investment, focusing on solid waste would generate benefits for each state worth around ₹2 for every rupee spent.

Finally, focusing on the urban water supply would mean even better returns.

Urban 24x7 piped water total costs and benefits

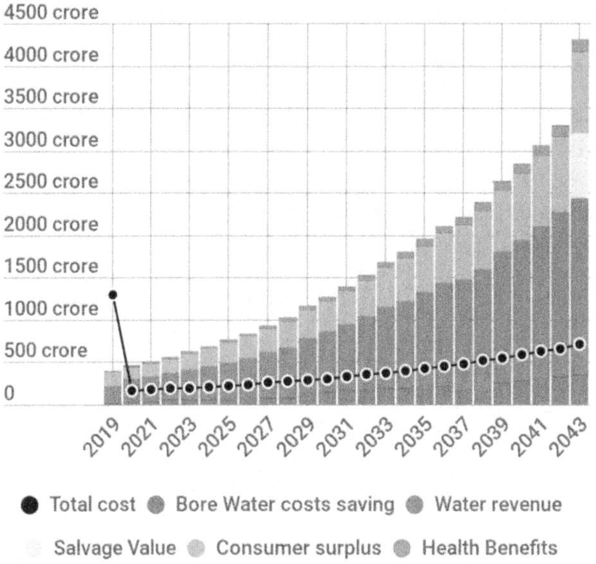

About 60 percent of households are connected, but 93% of residential connections are unconnected. For Vijayawada, supplying 100% coverage would mean replacing 80 percent of existing distribution pipes, and the costs would come to ₹5,481 crore.

Citizens would not only have health benefits (worth more than ₹800 crore alone), but would also be able to avoid the cost of creating bore well and pump maintenance to extract ground water. These advantages, plus revenues to the city, would mean benefits add up to ₹18,300 crore.

This suggests a return on investment worth more than three rupees.

What is clear is that India's cities are burgeoning, and significant infrastructure needs to be developed to meet unmet demand and to keep pace with the growth.

Interventions	BCR	Benefit	Cost
Urban 24x7 piped water supply	3.3	₹18,299 crore	₹5,481 crore
Urban sewerage and wastewater treatment 100 percent	2.1	₹2,824 crore	₹1,335 crore
Urban waste collection 100 percent	1.1	₹3,829 crore	₹3,385 crore

Total costs and benefits estimated over a 25-year time horizon and discounted at 5%

ANALYSING WATER AND SANITATION OPTIONS FOR THE STATE

Diarrheal disease caused nearly 1.7 million deaths globally in 2016. Nearly 0.8 million of these deaths occurred in India of which 90% were due to unsafe drinking water, sanitation and hygiene according to estimates by the Global Burden of Disease 2016. In Andhra Pradesh, more than 30,000 deaths were caused by diarrheal disease and intestinal infections (mainly typhoid and paratyphoid) in 2016, constituting 8% of all deaths in the state according to GBD 2016.

To address these issues, 4 interventions are analysed by economist Bjorn Larsen. Benefits and costs are presented as a ratio of annualized benefits and annualized costs over the expected useful life of each intervention.

About 73% of households in Andhra Pradesh had access to an improved drinking water source in 2015-16 according to the National Family Health Survey 4 (NFHS 4). Only 19% of households practiced point-of-use (POU) treatment of their drinking water in 2005-06 (Andhra Pradesh & Telangana), mainly by filtering (11%) and boiling (8%) (NFHS 3). Moreover, 14% of population in Andhra Pradesh (and Telangana) had more than 30 minutes round-trip to their drinking water source in 2005-06 (NFHS 3), particularly affecting women and children.

Providing urban households without an improved drinking water source with piped water to dwelling, or rural households with a tube well/borehole would cost ₹1,233 – 1,753 per household. This includes initial capital cost of piped water supply or tube well/borehole and annual operations and maintenance cost. For urban areas the annualized cost of improved drinking water supply is estimated at ₹228.02 crores per year and for rural areas annualized cost is estimated at ₹440.32 crores per year.

The intervention would benefit about 4.7 million households. The largest benefits are avoided mortality and productivity benefits in terms of time savings from water source closer to dwelling.

Households covered by proposed water interventions

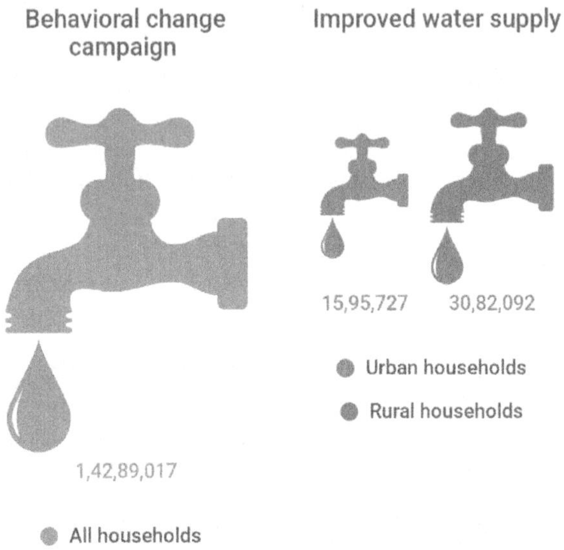

For urban intervention annualized benefits are estimated at ₹1,079 crores per year and for rural area annualized benefits are estimated at ₹1,135 crores per year.

Only 19% of households in Andhra Pradesh (and Telangana) practiced appropriate methods of point-of-use (POU) treatment of drinking water a decade ago, compared to over 20% nationwide in India according to the NFHS 3 (2005-06).

A behavioural change campaign that promotes household POU treatment of drinking water with a filter would cost 342.2 crores, targeting 1.4-2.8 million households (the cost for them to start POU treatment by filtering of drinking water has been factored). It is estimated that about 1,200-2,400 deaths and 2.6-5.1 million cases of diarrheal illness will be averted per year. Total value of the health and productivity benefits of the intervention is estimated at ₹1,035.6 crores per year.

About 61% of households in AP had a sanitary toilet facility in 2015 according to the Swachhta Status Report 2016. The most common household sanitation facility in Andhra Pradesh is a flush/pour-flush toilet in both urban and rural areas. Therefore, this intervention targets 95% household coverage with improved, non-shared sanitation is applied.

Households covered by proposed sanitation interventions

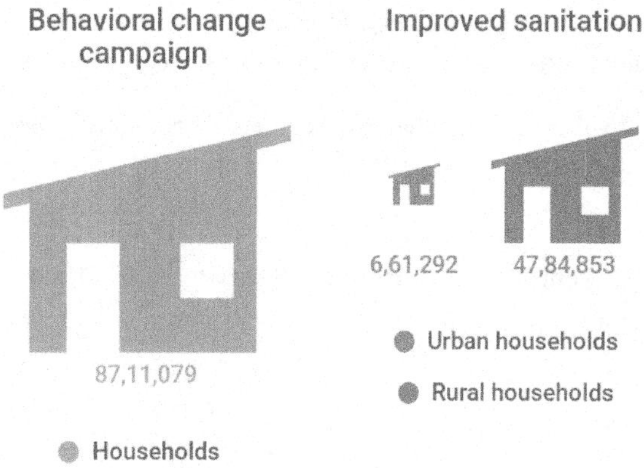

Costs of household sanitation include initial capital cost, periodic emptying of pit or septic tank (once in 5 years), annual operations and maintenance cost, cost or time for cleaning of sanitation facility, and cost of sanitation promotion programs by the government. The annualized cost per household is estimated at ₹5,577 for rural households and ₹8,229 for urban households. It is estimated that over 7,000 deaths and 15.4 million cases of diarrheal illness will be averted per year due to this intervention.

The total value of the annualized health and productivity benefits of the intervention is estimated at ₹2,199.6 crores for urban areas and ₹1,4201.1 crores for rural areas.

Finally, the researcher looks at promotion of the use of sanitation facilities. The Swachhta Status Report 2016 found that 2.2% of household members continue to practice Open Defecation after construction of sanitation facility. Non-use is more prevalent in rural areas (2.7%) than in urban areas (1.1%). The intervention is a behavioural change campaign that promotes the consistent use of existing sanitation facilities.

The total annualized cost (both BCC program and additional costs of improved water, etc) of this intervention is ₹67.4 crores. The intervention would end OD among 72-145 thousand household members. It is estimated cases of 14-28 deaths and about 30-61 thousand cases of diarrheal illness will be averted per year.

The total value of the annualized health and productivity benefits of the intervention is estimated at ₹95.9 crores.

Interventions	BCR	Benefit	Cost
Rural flush / pour-flush sanitation	5.3	₹14,201 crore / year	₹2,668.3 crore / year
Urban improved drinking water supply	4.7	₹1,079 crore / year	₹228.02 crore / year
Urban flush / pour-flush sanitation	4.0	₹2,200 crore / year	₹544.1 crore / year
Behavioural change for household treatment of drinking water	3.0	₹1,036 crore / year	₹342.2 crore / year
Rural improved drinking water supply	2.6	₹1,135 crore / year	₹440.32 crore / year
Behavioural change for use of existing sanitation facilities	1.4	₹95.9 crore / year	₹67.4 crore / year

Total costs and benefits estimated over a 25-year time horizon and discounted at 5%

Andhra Pradesh Priorities Eminent Panel Findings

The Andhra Pradesh Priorities Eminent Panel comprises:

- Nisha Agrawal
- Vinita Bali
- S Mahendra Dev
- Finn Kydland

The Eminent Panel sought to address the research proposals with a view to answering the question: *On which initiatives should additional resources be spent first?*

The Eminent Panel intends these findings to be informative not just to the Government of Andhra Pradesh, but also to others, including NGOs, the private sector and charitable organizations.

The panel examined the proposals in detail. Each proposal was discussed with its principal author. The panel was informed by Sector Expert Commentaries, and by Eminent Panel members' own critical appraisals and discussions on assumptions and methodology.

In ordering the proposals, the Eminent Panel was guided predominantly by consideration of social, economic and environmental costs and benefits.

The Eminent Panel acknowledged the difficulties that cost-benefit analysis must overcome, both in principle and as a practical matter, but agreed that the cost-benefit approach was a very important organizing method.

Each Eminent Panel member assigned his or her own ranking to proposals. The Eminent Panel's ranking was calculated by taking the median of individual rankings.

The Eminent Panel jointly endorses the median ordering as representing their agreed view.

RANKING OF PROPOSALS

The Eminent Panel considers and prioritizes specific proposals to respond to challenges. This is different from ranking the challenges themselves. A low ranking of a proposal does not mean that the problem it addresses should be considered unimportant.

The Ranking was calculated by taking the median of each Eminent Panel member's individual rankings. The Eminent Panel jointly endorses the median ordering as representing their agreed view. In due course, the Eminent Panel's individual commentaries shall be published in book form.

In setting priorities, the Eminent Panel has taken into account the strengths and weaknesses of the specific cost-benefit appraisals under review, and has given weight both to the institutional preconditions for success and to the demands of ethical or humanitarian importance.

Based on the costs and benefits of the solutions and their own assessment, the panel ranked the proposals, in descending order of desirability, as follows:

Rank	Proposal
1	Computer assisted learning at the right level
2	Micronutrients for pregnant women at ANC visits
3	Immunization camps in lagging districts
4	Education for complementary feeding and hand-washing
5	Secondary prevention of cardiovascular disease
6	Self-help groups against domestic violence
7	Group and teach children at the right level
8	Community mobilisation against domestic violence
9	Package of nutrition based interventions
10	Improved cyclone early warning systems
11	Improve land records digitisation
12	Tablets to reduce anaemia in adolescent girls

13	Supplementary food for mother and child
14	Diabetes screening and treatment
15	Hire local teachers to improve pre-school classes in AWCs
16	Certified seed production
17	Family planning for unmet need
18	Toilet provision for girls' secondary school enrolment
19	Bicycle transfer for girls' secondary school enrolment
20	Expand urban ambulance network
21	Improved maternal and neonatal health care
22	Conditional cash transfer for ANC visits
23	Improve private sector TB care
24	Improve private sector TB care and active case finding
25	Expand rural ambulance network
26	Cash incentives to attend pre-school classes in AWCs
27	Seafood certification for export
28	Build warehouses, storage and cold chain
29	Subsidised apprenticeships
30	Treatment for children with severe acute malnutrition
31	Drip irrigation and mulching in high value crops
32	Vocational training program
33	Connect rural households to national fibre optic network
34	Improved mobile phone advisory
35	Mass media breastfeeding promotion and counselling
36	Flush / Pour-flush sanitation - rural
37	Expand skill training for women
38	Indoor air pollution: Improved biomass cookstoves promotion
39	Cash transfer for girls' secondary school enrolment
40	Elevated bus line system
41	Improved drinking water supply - urban
42	Zig-zag brick kiln technology to reduce air pollution
43	Vertical shaft brick kiln technology to reduce air pollution
44	Flush / Pour-flush sanitation - urban

45	Behavioural change for household treatment of drinking water
46	Expand water use efficient irrigation
47	Improved drinking water supply - rural
48	Coastal economic zone
49	Well-structured incentives to teachers
50	Urban 24x7 piped water supply
51	Direct non-monetary incentives to reduce child marriage
52	In-situ slum redevelopment
53	Urban waste collection 100 percent
54	Expand poverty graduation and livelihood programs
55	Energy efficient agricultural water pumps
56	Double teacher-pupil ratio
57	Cervical cancer screening and treatment
58	Credit support to micro, small and medium enterprises
59	Expand Aadhaar based payments for MGNREGA
60	Upgrade agricultural power distribution
61	Mental health counselling in schools
62	Behavioural change for use of existing sanitation facilities
63	Indoor air pollution: Free LPG connection to poor households
64	Expand crop insurance coverage
65	Hiring centres for farm machinery
66	Local food processing
67	Urban metro rail system
68	Energy storage in commercial buildings - water
69	Energy storage in commercial buildings - hybrid salts
70	Private-public affordable housing projects
71	Subsidised do-it-yourself extension and construction
72	Urban sewerage and wastewater treatment 100 percent
73	Breast cancer screening and treatment
74	Training of teachers
75	Port infrastructure and hinterland connectivity
76	Indoor air pollution: LPG subsidy reduction by 50%
77	Farmer loan waivers

• **Improved mobile phone advisory (Agriculture):** The Eminent Panel notes that it is especially important at the implementation phase to ensure that distributed cellphones reach women, who are most responsible for farming. The intervention's impact could be limited if the technology is held only in the hands of the men of households.

• **Family planning for unmet need (Health Systems):** The Eminent Panel is concerned that the burden of family planning should not be left entirely to women. Changes are required to the behaviour of both men and women. There is a strong case for looking at family planning holistically within spouses.

• **Mass media breastfeeding promotion and counselling and Conditional cash transfer for ANC visits (Mother and Child Health):** The Eminent Panel finds that it is imperative to look for new, better interventions in this important area, and to close evidence gaps and increase the knowledge space, so there can be more and better solutions to choose from.

• **Improve land records digitisation (Ease of Doing Business):** The Eminent Panel encourages the consideration of transferring land ownership to women. Removing barriers to women's ownership and control of physical and financial assets would help to ensure the full and equal participation of men and women in the economy.

Commentary on the Rankings

by Nisha Agrawal

Nisha Agrawal has worked on poverty, inequality and development issues for more than three decades. She was the Chief Executive Officer of Oxfam, India, and worked with the World Bank on development issues for 18 years. Agrawal has experience working in countries in East Asia (Cambodia, Vietnam and Indonesia) and in East Africa (Tanzania, Kenya and Uganda). She has a Doctorate in Economics from the University of Virginia, USA. She has also worked as a Research Economist at the Impact Research Centre, University of Melbourne, Australia.

Final Rankings

The overall process of arriving at the final rankings was a robust one and builds confidence in the methodology used and the results produced. The papers were of a high quality and were easy to read and consistent in their methodology and presentations. They were delivered in a timely manner so that one had ample time to read them before the meeting. What also worked well was the interaction amongst the panellists and the high quality and diversity of the panel (sector expertise and experience, geography, gender and so on) so that one felt one was getting multiple perspectives on any given issue. There was adequate time provided for presentations and the discussions.

It is interesting that the top 10 smartest solutions for AP are all in either the social sectors (9 of them) or in disaster management (an early warning system for cyclones). These are the areas where AP (and India as a whole) is really lagging its peers and where efforts need to be made to catch up. The solutions being recommended are tried and tested (in either India or other developing countries) and, importantly, have high rates of return on the investments to be made (with cost-benefit ratios in the range of 15—62). Many of them are fairly easy to implement and would have immediate benefits. By and large, there was a consensus between the panellists on the rankings, and where there was not, there was certainly a sense that we could all live with the final rankings.

My Top Rankings

In my top 10 rankings, there are two that I would like to comment on—improve land records digitization and family planning. These are both interventions that would be highly beneficial ***if and only if*** **the gender implications** were fully considered and built into the design of the intervention. But unfortunately, both papers have failed to do that.

Improve Land Records Digitization--Property rights in India are highly skewed in favour of men and only about 10-15 percent of the property is owned by women. For women farmers (and farming today is largely done by women in many states) it would make a huge difference to their productivity and incomes to have their names on the land titles so that they could have easier access to inputs such as credit etc. Owing property is also very empowering and leads to lower levels of violence against women (see Bina Agarwal's work). At the time of digitization, it would be very easy to add the name of the spouse on the title so that property is jointly owned by men and women. This should be included in the recommendations of the paper.

Family Planning for Unmet Need--On family planning as well, there are serious gender issues to consider which the paper does not do. Female sterilization is the most used method in India, often carried out in unhygienic sterilization camps leading, in some cases, even to the death of the patients. Very little effort has been made to encourage men to share the burden of contraception in India, either through the use of condoms or male sterilization. One needs to look at these issues in more detail than has been done here and it should be recommended that men and women both share the burden of family planning.

My Bottom Rankings

In my bottom 10 rankings, I would like to comment on five that have high benefit cost ratios (CBRs) (shown in parentheses below) but have been ranked at the bottom because the CBRs don't provide the complete story and other issues need to be taken into account.

Well-Structured Incentives to Teachers (15) –The problem with teachers' performance in India is not related to their poor incentives. Teachers are relatively well paid and have secure jobs and other benefits as public servants. They lack accountability, however, and wield a lot of power, not only because they are unionised but also because they perform many other useful roles for politicians and bureaucrats such as during elections, and so on. Just improving incentives without improving accountability will not serve much.

Vocational Training Program (16) –Good ***publicly run*** vocational training programs are hard to organize because the relevance of the training and the link to the labor market is missing and many times they end up creating a mis-match between demand and supply of skills. Also it is not clear if skills are a public good that should be funded by the public sector or a private good to be funded by the private sector. The government has recently stopped a massive skill development program that was to be delivered in public-private partnership mode because of various challenges. The design and implementation challenges of this program are tremendous and need to be taken into account.

Improve private sector TB care and active case finding (109) and Improve Private Sector TB Care (117) –Detecting and treating TB is something that primary health centers can do—and do do the world over-- and this study does not compare the CBR of doing this through the public health services. In India, 80% of health services are already in the private sector and only 20% in the public sector. The public sector is weak in quality because it has been starved of funds. India spends about 0.9% of GDP on public health care, one of the lowest in the world. The private sector in unregulated and delivers poor quality services for the poor. An alternative to further privatization is strengthening public service delivery and this option should also have been examined.

Expand UID (Aadhaar) based payments fort MGNREGA (11) –The UID was meant to a be a voluntary ID system but has slowly become almost mandatory in India and the Government has been attempting to link all kinds of services, especially those designed for poor people, to the Aadhaar card. There are several issues of concern, including those of privacy, since the database is a very leaky one. But there are also issues of concern about linking basic legal rights—like the rights to food or education or employment (through MGNREGA) —that are guaranteed by law to having an ID card. There are also many practical problems for poor people when the biometrics don't work and they are denied their essential services as a result, including their right to food, medical services and so on, leading to extreme hardship and, in some cases, death.

COMMENTARY ON THE RANKINGS
BY VINITA BALI

> Vinita Bali is a global business leader with extensive experience in leading large Companies in India and overseas. She has worked with The Coca-Cola Company and Cadbury Schweppes PLC in the UK, Nigeria, South Africa, USA and Latin America, in addition to Britannia Industries Ltd in India. She is a Non-Executive Director on the global boards of Smith & Nephew plc, and Bunge Ltd; and Chairman of GAIN (Global Alliance for Improved Nutrition). She served on the Global Board of Syngenta International AG from April 2012 to June 2017. In India, Vinita serves as a Non-Executive Director on the Boards of CRISIL Ltd and Syngene International Ltd; is a Member of the Board of Governors of Indian Institute of Management – Bangalore; and an Advisory Board Member of PricewaterhouseCoopers.

Based on a fairly intense discussion, following in-depth work done by economists and other domain experts from India and overseas, on 77 possible interventions for Andhra Pradesh, the 3 themes that emerged as the most important had to do with Education & Learning, Nutrition & Health and Gender Sensitivity.

The long list of proposed interventions included several other relevant initiatives that addressed specific problems and challenges that AP faces in various areas, e.g., agricultural practices – like lack of mechanisation & irrigation etc., that result in low productivity; outdoor & indoor air pollution; inadequate urban infrastructure; poor sanitation; child marriage; prevalence of communicable diseases like tuberculosis, etc. It was a hard choice for panel members, even though the benefit-cost analyses were clear.

Overall, the Panel concluded, after significant discussion that covered a diversity of perspectives, that unless the basics of better Nutrition, better Education and a heightened awareness to deal with Gender Sensitive issues (like domestic violence) are addressed, systemic and enduring progress will remain elusive and, in fact, some of the other interventions may have limited traction. Additionally, the Panel agreed that even though interventions like improving private sector TB care had the highest benefit-cost ratio, the way to address those should be to focus on improving the public delivery of better TB care, rather than shifting its responsibility to the private sector.

Thematically, the top 10 interventions stack up as follows:

Education

- Computer assisted learning at the right level #1
- Group and teach children at the right level #7

Nutrition & Health

- Micronutrients for pregnant women at ANC visits #2
- Education for complementary feeding and hand-washing #4
- Package of nutrition based interventions #9
- Immunisation camps in lagging districts #3
- Secondary prevention of cardiovascular disease #5

Gender Sensitivity

- Self-help groups against domestic violence #6
- Community mobilisation against domestic violence #8

And, at #10 was the investment in cyclone early warning systems to avoid losses in this particular geography where cyclones and frequent.

To some extent, this also reflects the conviction of the Panel and therefore, its approach, to addressing systemic issues with requisite interventions, sequenced and paced in a certain hierarchy, and where the cost benefit is a significant, but not the only factor. The challenge is to balance the benefits and cost with the priority and significance of the issue itself.

I found the well informed and healthy discussion on the importance and significance of gender sensitivity very productive, given the skewed emphasis on addressing basic issues of equity and fairness, with respect to women and girls. Domestic violence that finds its way into very long and dominant inequities and perpetuation of misogynistic mind-sets with respect to the significance and contribution of women was considered to be a key issue which if not addressed, would continue aggression and violence against women and girls. Its benefit-cost ratio of 22 has provided a compelling reason for it to be in the Top 10 initiatives.

In my own case, some of the Nutrition interventions featured right on top, given that poor Nutrition is both a social inequity as well as an economic burden, in that it leads to lower productivity and ultimately GDP loss. My ranking of interventions was also influenced by the belief that if the foundational factors are not conducive, sustainable progress is hard to achieve and those foundational factors had to do with Nutrition, Education and Gender Equity, within which all interventions had a positive and compelling cost benefit outcomes. Additionally, as the most vulnerable segments of under-nutrition happen to be women and children, addressing their basic needs also improves overall health outcomes of communities.

It was hard to exclude several initiates related to improvement in agriculture and agricultural productivity from the top 10, which also highlights the dilemma of resource allocation in an environment of finite resources. The bottom 10 interventions on my list had to do with either relatively lower cost-benefit ratios (4 interventions were less than 1.0) and others, like well-structured incentives to teachers or doubling the teacher-pupil ratio, in my perspective, were not as convincing in their implementation capability.

Finally, this entire process – the detailed work done each intervention, and the discussions that followed, highlighted a poignant fact of India's economic growth – in that, economic growth alone will not take care of the large inequities of our diverse and heterogeneous population, unless human development is explicitly and overtly made part of the economic development agenda.

Commentary on the Rankings

by S. Mahendra Dev

S Mahendra Dev is Vice Chancellor of Indira Gandhi Institute for Development Research. He is Consultant and Adviser to many international organizations, including the United Development Programme, the World Bank, and the International Labor Organisation. Dev was Chairman of the Commission for Agricultural Costs and Prices, Ministry of Agriculture, in the rank of Secretary to Government of India from 2008 to 2010, and Acting Chairman of the National Statistical Commission of India in the rank of Minister of State. From 1999 to 2008, he was Director of the Centre for Economic and Social Studies in Hyderabad, India. He is President of the Indian Economic Association, Vice Chairman of Board of Trustees of IFPRI, and Chairman of the Committee on Terms of Trade on Agriculture constituted by the Indian Ministry of Agriculture.

I have enjoyed participating in the Eminent Panel event in Vijayawada, Andhra Pradesh. The event was organised very well. We got all the studies well in advance so that one could go through them thoroughly. I have also enjoyed interaction with my fellow panellists, the paper presenters, representatives from Tata Trust and Copenhagen Consensus.

Methodology

At the outset, I may mention that the eminent panel members have read the papers including methodology of calculating the benefit cost ratio. One can comment on the components of costs and benefits. In general, we did not raise methodological issues as they are straightforward cost benefit calculations.

On final rankings of the Panel

I agree with the final rankings of the eminent panel. If we take first 20 ranks, they cover sectors like education, health, nutrition, women, cyclone warning systems, land records, certified seeds in agriculture. The panel has rightly given importance to these crucial sectors to improve the socio, economic and environmental development of the state. Panel also thinks that government plays an important role in sectors like health and education while private sector role would be useful in areas like solid waste management in urban areas.

Each study provides the BCRs for the identified interventions. However, most of the studies say that the rankings based on BCRs should not be taken as mutually exclusive but to be taken complementarily prioritising the investments. As one paper puts it all the interventions "may produce many types of externalities not accounted for" in the analysis and estimation of benefit-cost ratios' (Shariff and Amit Sharma). However, the panel, in general, respected the benefit cost ratio approach.

Procedure followed by me in ranking:

(1) I gave importance to the sectors like education, health, nutrition, women etc. in giving preference over other interventions even though some of the benefit cost ratios are low. For example, after the first rank intervention, I gave ranks 2,3,4,5 to all nutrition interventions as we need them as a package. In the case of intervention on 'package of nutrition based interventions', the BCR is only 9. But I gave 5th rank because of its importance.

(2) Also gave importance to government interventions in sectors like health, education and nutrition. For example, the two interventions on TB have the highest BCRs of 117 and 109. But, I included them somewhere after 20 ranks and gave 27 and 28 ranks. This is because it mainly relates to private interventions.

(3) The study on land records is not very convincing. I have given 11th rank instead of third rank based on BCRs.

(4) I also gave slightly higher ranks to the interventions on adolescents, child marriage and early child development because of their importance.

(5) The intervention on 'treatment for children with severe acute malnutrition' has BCR of 4 only. I moved it up to 34th rank as I felt this intervention was useful.

(6) The rank for intervention on 'coastal economic zone' got less rank as the study was not convincing. Implementation is also a problem.

(7) The intervention on 'Breast Cancer screening and treatment' relating to NCDs has the lowest BCR of 0.4 among

77 interventions. I moved it up to 61st rank as it is important intervention.

(8) For rest of the interventions, I followed the ranks based on BCRs.

To sum up, in general I respected the BCR approach. Though the ranking is done majorly following the BCRs, I deviated in some cases giving primacy to the basic sectors of Health, Education, Nutrition and Women. Deviation is also based on the quality of the studies (which are less convincing) and implementation difficulties. I also gave preference to government interventions in sectors like education and health. Political aspects and feasibility are not considered while ranking. While it is easier to rank the interventions within the sector, ranking them across sectors all put together is a slightly daunting task.

My reasoning for top and bottom interventions

(1) I gave top rank to intervention on 'computer assisted learning at the right level' relating to education sector as the latter is the crucial sector and it has got the highest BCR

(2) Intervention on 'Farm loan waivers' relating to farm distress is given bottom rank for obvious reasons. Most of the politicians favour this intervention. But, economically it is not a solution for removing farmer's distress.

(3) I gave the first ten ranks to sectors on education, nutrition, health, crime and violence against women and early warning system. It matches more or less with the eminent panel ranking.

(4) The bottom ten rankings are more or less based on BCRs with some tinkering like the intervention of farm loan waivers getting the last rank of 77.

(5) Some of the sectors like WASH, urban infrastructure, energy storage, air pollution etc. are equally important but they got low benefit cost ratios.

Way forward: As mentioned in the meetings with Chief Minister, Chief Secretary and Secretaries, the way forward is preparing action plan. For example, nutrition interventions can be strengthened. Similarly women's self-help groups can be used to reduce domestic violence. Also the interventions have to take into account regional disparities as the averages mask these variations. Three regions viz., North Coastal, South Coastal and Rayalaseema have different socio-economic problems. Some of the interventions may not be relevant for all the regions.

To conclude, I thoroughly enjoyed the eminent panel event and learned a lot. In general I agree with the 'low hanging fruit' approach and getting highest benefit for one rupee of investment. It is now up to the government to take it forward.

COMMENTARY ON THE RANKINGS

BY FINN KYDLAND

Finn Kydland is a Norwegian-born economist known for his contributions to business cycle theory. He is the Henley Professor of Economics at the University of California, Santa Barbara. He also holds the Richard P. Simmons Distinguished Professorship at the Tepper School of Business of Carnegie Mellon University, where he earned his Ph.D., and a part-time position at the Norwegian School of Economics. Kydland was a co-recipient of the 2004 Nobel Memorial Prize in Economics, with Edward C. Prescott, "for their contributions to dynamic macroeconomics: the time consistency of economic policy and the driving forces behind business cycles".

General methodology and criteria

Andhra Pradesh is the most recently formed state in India with a 50 million population and separated from Telangana, its northern neighbour, in 2014. Andhra Pradesh Priorities is a prioritization project within the India Consensus Partnership between the Copenhagen Consensus Center and Tata Trusts. Like other parts of the developing world, this new state faces social and economic development challenges. This document describes the top five and bottom five public policies –out of 75 interventions in 28 sectors to help Andhra Pradesh to solve these challenges.

The top five interventions were chosen based on the following criteria: a low number of implementation concerns, the self-assessment of quality of the evidence, the benefit-cost ratios, and if they were aimed at vulnerable populations or not. Interventions that score high in all these components were more likely to be in the top five policies. Similarly, the solutions that score low in the four criteria are more likely to be in the bottom five. It is not sufficient to have a high benefit-cost ratio to be in the five top programs. For example, a policy with a high benefit-cost ratio, but that has a high number of implementation concerns or for which the quality of evidence is low is less likely to be in the top five.

Implementation concerns are related to unintended consequences of public policy. Unintended consequences could be positive or negative but tend to be negative. They can be realized as an externality over a group that was not targeted originally, or even as a consequence to the same group that the policy initially focused. They may relate to general equilibrium effects. Implementation concerns are similarly associated with the uncertainty of foreseen benefits, which may be lower, or costs, which may be higher.

A specific benefit-cost ratio (BCR) implies that for every dollar or rupee spent on a program, the benefits are a factor of the BCR. This indicator allows comparing multiple policies targeted to different populations or sectors. BCRs do not depend on the original unit of measure of benefits or costs. A BCR higher than one implies that the policy has a positive impact. Similarly, a BCR lower than one means that a solution is "losing money," i.e., it invests some value and recovers less than the original investment. A BCR of 1 means that the policy breaks even, i.e., benefits and costs are the same.

Our top five policies usually target vulnerable populations. For instance, Andhra Pradesh still has a considerable percentage of children suffering from stunting, and a majority of women in reproductive age are anaemic. Examples of such policies include micronutrients to pregnant women; improved tuberculosis care and screening; and increased immunization in lagging districts.

Top five programs

The list of our high-ranked five interventions includes micronutrients for pregnant women at antenatal care (ANC) visits; improve private sector tuberculosis care and active case finding; immunization camps in lagging districts; prevention of cardiovascular disease (CVD); and computer-assisted learning at the right level.

The provision of micronutrients, including vitamin A, iron, iodine, calcium, zinc and folic acid, will help Andhra Pradesh to reduce the still high incidence of stunting of children and anaemia in women in reproductive age. Mothers will receive the micronutrients in antenatal care visits. The response will help break the vicious intergenerational cycle of undernutrition and will guarantee safe motherhood. Future programs will account for possible decreasing effects of additional nutrition interventions or "cannibalization" effects between programs. Cannibalization may happen because further solutions do not increase benefits in the same percentage as costs rise.

It is worth noting that a benefit not considered in the study for Andhra Pradesh is the potential value of this intervention as a stepping stone for a follow-up of micronutrients for the children in the first two years of their lives, with significant reductions in stunting. A controlled trial of nutritional supplements in Guatemala, in which the subjects were followed up two or three decades later, suggests that especially the human capital portion of the benefits would be strengthened significantly. The results for Guatemala are sufficiently dramatic to make this follow-up also for Andhra Pradesh a potentially extremely beneficial part of this intervention.

We consider as one of our top five policies the secondary prevention of CVD through the use of a multidrug poly-pill. This program is aimed at the population aged 30-69 and assessed as being at high risk, and at those with existing CVD. The target will be to screen 70% of this population with the assumption of achieving 60% adherence to treatment. Global Burden of Disease (2017) estimates that CVD causes 487/100,000 deaths in AP, of which about 20% could be averted with the suggested regimen.

Likewise, the policy to promote private sector engagement combined with slum-case finding of tuberculosis is part of our top interventions. Currently, patients will seek care in private providers before going into the public sector which has higher quality standards. If the scheme can increase the capacity of the private sector to diagnose and treat tuberculosis, the gains concerning deaths and years without a disability are huge -the BCR is 102. Moreover, the private sector has already invested in facilities that otherwise the government has to build if public provision is to be expanded. This policy's central mechanism does not only include the direct benefits to patients but to the potential tuberculosis cases that would otherwise have developed. The costs amount to ₹35.2 crore per year in 2018-2049, and the expected benefits are 3,454 fewer deaths per year (15.9% fewer deaths that otherwise would have occurred).

We observe the immunization of children as a policy to prioritize. The current system of providing vaccination for children is insufficient especially in remote areas. The intervention will make AP attain India's immunization rate (from 55 to 65%) using in-kind transfers (lentils and meals) after spending ₹10 crore (of which 74% corresponds to incentives). This solution closely follows a randomized control trial implemented in Rajasthan, which concludes that it is more cost effective than merely increasing immunization supply. The strategy will save the lives of 219 children per year and prevent 5,946 years lived with a disability (YLDs).

Finally, computer-assisted learning at the right level is the last policy in our top five. Andhra Pradesh has increased the enrolment of children in school, but it is lagging in the quality of education. The proposed intervention aims to use a personalized multiplatform software, in the spirit of Mindspark, to increase the students' learning outcomes. The software will require support in multiple languages so more students can benefit. An expected increase of lifetime stream of income will make it possible to attain a BCR of 62.

Bottom five programs

On the other hand, the bottom five programs share in common the low quality of the evidence, implementation concerns, and low benefit-cost ratios. These include the farm loan waiver; port infrastructure and hinterland connectivity; Indoor air pollution: liquefied petroleum gas (LPG) subsidy reduction by 50%; expand crop insurance coverage; and local food processing units.

The farm loan waiver program proposes to invest ₹23,300 crore to bail out small farmers. The literature has found that the benefits do not compensate the costs (BCR is lower than 1), which include higher moral hazard and loss of the credit discipline, i.e., increased non-performing loans and defaults possibly connected to the political cycle. Similarly, evidence shows that after bailout the probability of getting credit is lower, which further causes production drops and livelihoods reductions. Benefits include the direct payment for each landholder and an increased credit expansion for more prominent farmers.

Modernizing port facilities and improving hinterland connectivity is one of the bottom policies. The project seeks an increase in port infrastructure through the acquisition of 1000 acres of land. Access to credit might be a problem since Indian banks currently have high non-performing loans. Not only is the BCR of the project less than 1, but also the project considers to use private investment jointly with public resources. We know that the private sector may prefer profitable ventures, so it is very likely that any government amounts of money spent on this project are invested in the less cost-effective areas.

A reduction in retail price subsidies to LPG is part of our bottom five list. Although subsidies create market distortions, the benefit of this policy is to avoid deaths and years lived with a disability attributed to respiratory diseases, to households that otherwise would not use LPG. We consider that further gains are possible if the scheme could identify how to protect more impoverished families while allowing better off ones to pay market prices. These subsidies have implications for government finances, especially, when households consume more LPG as they become wealthier.

We place crop insurance as part of the bottom five policies. This program subsidizes 98% of insurance premiums to farmers. The program lacks coverage (only 21.8% of cropped area), and generates moral hazard because farmers will cultivate in the regions that are prone to natural disasters despite higher theoretical yields. The scheme may not serve the most vulnerable population since there are no caps on the insured amount per farmer. The program is relatively costly (₹21 billion), and its benefit-cost ratio is modestly low (1.36.)

Finally, we consider that the policy of setting up more food processing units is part of the bottom five programs. The study is not clear about what constitutes a local, small-scale food processing unit. Two studies from the neighbouring states of Karnataka and Tamil Nadu suggest that the benefit-cost ratio is 1 for rice, and 4 for turmeric. The program does not aggregate these numbers into a single indicator weighting by either the current or future added value of these crops. The benefits and costs are not provided. We conclude that the current formulation of this policy is very uncertain and should not be prioritized.

Next Steps

The findings of the Andhra Pradesh Priorities Eminent Panel help establish which investments would do the most social, environmental and economic good in Andhra Pradesh for every rupee spent.

The Eminent Panel of Finn Kydland, Mahendra Dev, Vinita Bali, and Nisha Agrawal provide valuable food for thought, and a valuable policy-making input.

Their findings, presented over previous pages, speak for themselves – but it is useful to delve into some of the most important investments that they highlighted.

Two education interventions are among the top-ten priorities chosen by the Eminent Panel: teaching children in groups at the right level, and computer-assisted learning. Researchers from Sunay Policy Advisory found that a rupee spent on these could achieve more than sixty rupees in benefits, by improving life-long earnings.

As Professor Kydland said during the Eminent Panel, "Andhra Pradesh has successfully lifted school enrolment and retention rates. To achieve its full potential, it is crucial to focus on lifting educational quality. The Andhra Pradesh Priorities Eminent Panel heard strong evidence that there are relatively cheap approaches that would lift test scores and improve life-long earnings." The research presented to the panel – and included in this book – makes it clear that there is a strong rationale to zero in on this area.

And two nutrition efforts – improving micronutrient provision at ANC visits, and an education campaign to promote hand-washing – also appear among the top-ten priorities, based on the research by the Institute of Economic Growth, Delhi showing phenomenal returns to society, worth 40-60 times investment.

Vinita Ball summed up the Eminent Panel's thinking by saying, "Andhra Pradesh has made satisfactory progress in mother and child nutrition, but the Eminent Panel's findings underline the need to continue this focus, given the fairly high incidence of stunting, wasting and underweight children. The toll from poor nutrition and poor hygiene and sanitation remains far too high, and there is a forceful case to be made for prioritizing effective nutrition policies."

And based on the evidence encapsulated in this book on the costs of gender-based violence to Andhra Pradesh from researchers from National University of Ireland, Galway, the Eminent Panel gave high priority to two domestic violence approaches that have been shown to reduce violence: a self help group-based intervention for combating violence against women, and a community mobilisation programme.

Dr Nisha Agrawal noted, "it is extremely concerning that nearly one-in-two married women in Andhra Pradesh experience violence, and that domestic violence rates in the state are increasing. It's vital that we recognise that economic growth does not automatically lead to a reduction in violence. Resources need to be devoted to initiatives that have been proven to change gender norms and behaviour, such as those looked at by Andhra Pradesh Priorities researchers. As a human rights issue, a health issue, and an economic issue, domestic violence must be a priority."

Looking across all of the top-ten initaitives, as Professor S. Mahendra Dev noted, we see nutrition, mother-and-child health, and immunisation approaches that all have huge potential to benefit the state: "Focusing on improving maternal and infant health can transform entire lives. This is an area where effective interventions can achieve a lot of value for every rupee spent. By improving nutrition and lifting immunisation coverage, Andhra Pradesh can help to ensure that increasing opportunities for the next generation are more broadly shared. Nutrition improvements have both intrinsic and instrumental values. This can improve the human development of the people and enhance GSDP of the state."

The Eminent Panel's findings are important – but it's important to note that prioritisation is something for everyone, not just renowned economists. We have published our research in state and national newspapers to broaden this conversation – and that is why we are publishing this book.

Ultimately, we look forward to continuing our close cooperation with the state government and with local stakeholders. We are very interested in continuing to work with Andhra Pradesh to help make sure that this research translates into action that can offer value-for-money policies that help boost the state's social development and economic potential.

Since the Eminent Panel, there has been a very promising response from the state government.

The entire Eminent Panel, along with the Andhra Pradesh Priorities team, met the Hon'ble Chief Minister of AP - N. Chandrababu Naidu - at his residence in Vijayawada on the evening of 20th June 2018.

The Chief Minister welcomed the findings presented in this book, and told us that he intended to continuously work with the project team. He said, "it's a very good study and I am very happy with it. I invite Andhra Pradesh Priorities to present an Action Plan for implementation."

That is exactly what we continue to work on. No government has unlimited funds, and prioritisation based on the principle of cost-benefit analysis can help to identify policies that make every rupee go further. It is to be hoped that this new evidence is used to help to shape decision-making in Andhra Pradesh, for the betterment of all in the state.

REFLECTIONS ON THE FINDINGS: THE USE AND UTILISATION OF THIS RESEARCH

BY R. PAVITHRA KUMAR

Since the inception of Tata Trusts, the organisation has played a leading role in transforming traditional ideas of charity and introducing the concept of philanthropy to make a real difference to communities across India.

Through grant-making, direct implementation and co-partnership strategies, the Trusts support and drive innovation in a myriad of areas, including healthcare and nutrition; water and sanitation; energy; education; rural livelihoods; natural resource management; urban poverty alleviation; enhancing civil society and governance; media, arts, crafts and culture; and diversified employment.

In addition to promoting and facilitating initiatives in elementary education, Tata Trusts also award fellowships and merit scholarships to students pursuing higher studies. It grooms social scientists, cancer specialists, nuclear scientists and distinguished institutional administrators, who in turn have striven to make the country a power to reckon with in various fields, including science and technology.

The Trusts also support causes and initiatives that provide disaster relief and aids in rescue work in case of calamities. The Trusts not only assist by providing grants and helping to mobilise funds, they also offer on-ground support directly as well as in partnership with other stakeholders.

With such a broad approach, the Trusts have long had the approach of engaging with leaders in many fields, including researchers, government bodies, international agencies and like-minded private sector organisations, to nurture a self-sustaining eco-system that collectively works within every one of the areas in which the philanthropy engages.

This approach has extended to our partnership with the Copenhagen Consensus Center and with the researchers whose work is presented in this book. Tata Trusts developed and fostered these relationships with the motivation to ensure that state governments and many other interested parties are provided with cutting-edge analysis on approaches to solving the biggest challenges of today.

That is because of our enduring belief that one of the most important contributions that the Trusts can make is to significantly contribute to building intellectual capital and the knowledge base in the country.

This approach is underpinned by the belief that evidence and analysis is a crucial input to decision-making of any sort. And when it comes to philanthropy or government-spending, it is especially wise to look closely at what each rupee achieves, to maximise the returns to society and ensure that investment leads to results.

This project has, to date, produced research that allows for insights that can lead to better-informed decision-making.

It is an important principle that the Trusts share this knowledge freely with other philanthropies, corporations, researchers, government organisations, and—perhaps most importantly--state governments across India.

Ensuring that relevant state governments can avail themselves of this research is just one step in a multifaceted program of engagement that includes providing technical support, along with adapting and updating this research to ensure that it can best and most meaningfully be utilised.

State governments are in many ways the engine room of India's future progress, so it is crucial that they are fully empowered with the evidence and knowledge to make well-informed decisions.

We are very heartened and encouraged by the Rajasthan planning department advising its various state departments to act on the priorities and by the request from the Andhra Pradesh Chief

Minister for an action plan based on the research presented in this book.

The research presented in this book, whether on how to build educational outcomes, improve health results, lift economic performance, or enhance environmental wellbeing, contains such evidence that, collectively or individually, can be taken up by state governments, and other organisations, to be utilised in ways that improve the decision-making process.

An additional important potential audience is to be found within the private sector of India. Through corporate social responsibility (CSR) programmes, businesses can be at the forefront of finding ways to make a positive difference within the communities they inhabit and work alongside.

Innovative CSR has great potential to enhance community wellbeing, owing to enabling government legislation that has created the ecosystem for proper engagement. It is important, though, that CSR funds are spent just as wisely as any other money spent by a business, in order to ensure that this is sustainable and / or meaningful.

For those working in this space, looking carefully at the findings presented by this project, whether within a topic or across all subjects, can be a very fruitful starting point for prudent CSR management.

With close to 1,000 + projects being executed through 700+ partners, Tata Trusts reached millions of households across India. This is a broad remit, meaning that knowledge generation and sharing, from one community and state to another, is at the heart of developing a knowledge base that can be usefully applied.

This research can enhance that mission, and can be utilised in ways that will ensure that lessons are learned from success stories around India—and to applying those lessons wisely.

R. Pavithra Kumar
Director – Program Design, Tata Trusts

Made in the USA
Monee, IL
04 November 2026

67382308R00079